Simple **Kayak**
Navigation

Simple *Kayak* Navigation

Practical Piloting for the Passionate Paddler

Ray Killen

RAGGED MOUNTAIN PRESS / McGRAW-HILL

CAMDEN, MAINE • NEW YORK
CHICAGO • SAN FRANCISCO • LISBON
LONDON • MADRID • MEXICO CITY
MILAN • NEW DELHI • SAN JUAN
SEOUL • SINGAPORE
SYDNEY • TORONTO

To Margaret, my wife and kayaking partner.
May you always be by my side.

The McGraw·Hill Companies

1 2 3 4 5 6 7 8 9 DOC DOC 9 8 7 6

Library of Congress Cataloging-in-Publication Data
Killen, Ray.
Simple kayak navigation : practical piloting for passionate paddlers / Ray Killen.
    p.   cm.
Includes bibliographical references and index.
ISBN 0-07-146794-7 (pbk. : alk. paper)
1. Kayak touring. 2. Navigation. I. Title.
GV789.K55 2006
797.122'4—dc22   2006001075

All photos by Ray and Margaret Killen.
Illustrations by Ben White and Techbooks.

Questions regarding the content of this book should be addressed to
Ragged Mountain Press
P.O. Box 220
Camden, ME 04843
www.raggedmountainpress.com

Questions regarding the ordering of this book should be addressed to
The McGraw-Hill Companies
Customer Service Department
P.O. Box 547
Blacklick, OH 43004
Retail customers: 1-800-262-4729
Bookstores: 1-800-722-4726

Contents

Acknowledgments

FIRST AND FOREMOST, I WOULD LIKE TO THANK MY WIFE, MARGARET, for giving me the encouragement, support, and freedom to pursue just about anything I've wanted to do. I would also like to give my sincere thanks to Rita Romeu, PhD, for taking time from her busy schedule to offer constructive criticism.

Gabriel Romeu, ACA Coastal Kayak Instructor, has also donated much of his time. Many suggestions and comments offered by him have made it into this book.

A big thanks to Ben Fuller, curator at the Penobscot Marine Museum in Searsport, Maine, and an instructor in small craft seamanship, for his valuable comments.

Special thanks to Tim Williams, teacher and ACA Coastal Kayak Instructor, for tracking down all the online navigation resources.

I am also indebted to all the ACA Coastal Kayak Instructors whom I have certified for keeping me on my toes. During the many days we have spent together in my workshops, I have learned as much from you as you have from me.

Finally, I would like to thank all the authors who have previously written about navigation. It is your wide assortment of writing and teaching styles that has allowed me to learn something from each of you. Indeed, without your books, I would not have learned much at all.

Introduction

SEA KAYAKING MEANS DIFFERENT THINGS TO DIFFERENT PEOPLE. SOME enjoy paddling on small lakes, rivers, and estuaries. Others may paddle on larger bays or perhaps on the ocean—a dynamic, unpredictable environment. Wind, waves, currents, fog, tides, and other such variables make sea kayaking the interesting, enjoyable, and challenging sport it is. In fact, without this, many paddlers would consider kayaking dull. However, it also demands diligence and skill, requiring you to continually pay attention, make adjustments, and compensate as you paddle.

My purpose in writing this book is to teach you basic navigational skills—skills that will help you get where you want to go and keep you safe while getting there. Learning navigation requires an investment of your time. And knowing how valuable that time can be, I've chosen to focus this book on the basics: tides and currents, using a compass, handling wind and fog, being prepared, and a basic understanding of GPS receivers. With this information you should be able to plan a trip, follow your course, locate your position whenever necessary, and stay safe.

Although an important element, navigation is only one aspect of sea kayaking. I urge you to acquire a thorough knowledge of *all* aspects of the sport: correct paddling technique, proper equipment and clothing, the marine environment, safety measures, rescues, and most importantly, good judgment. Read other books and take classes, courses, or seminars to gain a broader understanding of this complex sport. The more informed and knowledgeable you are the safer you will be when you paddle.

While some kayakers only paddle in areas they are familiar with, others seek to explore, discover new destinations, and expand their skills. To do this safely and successfully means knowing how to navigate. Challenging? Certainly. But it's exciting as well. My aim is to teach you these skills and encourage you to venture out. What better time to start than now?

Getting Started

WHAT IS NAVIGATION?

NAVIGATION IS THE PROCESS OF DETERMINING WHERE you are at any given time when traveling from point A to point B. Every navigational decision depends upon you knowing your position. At minimum, you will need to know how to read a chart, use a compass, estimate your speed, and predict wind and currents.

There are three types of navigation a kayaker can use: 1) piloting, 2) dead reckoning, and 3) electronic (such as Global Positioning System). Chapter 9 is devoted to GPS; we'll cover piloting and dead reckoning below.

Piloting

To navigate by piloting is to use known landmarks and references to determine your position.

Picture this. You're riding in a car heading north on the Interstate. You pass a sign informing you that Route 72 is two miles ahead. Looking at the map, you see where the two roads intersect. You can now pinpoint where you are—two miles south of that intersection. You have used known landmarks and references to find your location. If you look further north on the map, you can see the town you are going to. Now you can estimate when you will arrive because you know the distance, speed, and direction.

"I understand that part, Ray," you say, "but what is piloting on the water?"

It's the same thing. When paddling along a familiar coast, for example, you recognize objects from previous trips. These objects let you know where you are, where you've just been, and where you are going. In areas that are unfamiliar, you use a

Your view of the lighthouse from buoy Number "4."

chart—which is what we call the map of the waterways. Instead of street signs, highway overpasses, and exit ramps, your landmarks become water towers, bridges, buildings, headlands, piers, buoys, and so on. In fact, anything you can see from the water that appears on your chart is a landmark.

For example, say you are paddling northeast toward a lighthouse and come upon a buoy with the number "4" on it (see illustration at left).

To find your position, look at your chart. Since you know you're close to the buoy, and you know you are pointing toward the lighthouse, you can determine precisely where you are and which way you're heading. Even if you didn't have a compass on your deck, you could estimate your heading from the clues on the chart (see illustration on following page).

Another, more-advanced method of piloting is to locate two objects that appear on a chart, take bearings to them, and plot those bearings on your chart. The intersection of those lines is your position. This is called a fix or fixing your position. I will show you how to do this in Chapter 2.

Dead Reckoning

If you have no landmarks in sight to fix your position, you can still get your approximate location by using other data, namely, your direction and the distance you've traveled. This process is called *dead reckoning*, which is basically an educated guess.

Let's get back in the car for a moment. Let's say you've been driving west for a half hour across the 50-mile span of open plains between the towns of Lastown and Nextown. Looking around you, you see no landmarks that you can use to locate your position on the map. How do you determine approximately where you are, and how can you estimate the distance to the next town?

"Let's see," you think. "I'm traveling due west at a speed of 70 miles per hour. In 30 minutes, I would have traveled half of 70 or 35 miles; therefore, I must be 35 miles due west of Lastown, with 15 miles to go before I get to Nextown."

To determine your position with any reasonable degree of accuracy in this instance, you need to know how long you've been traveling, your approximate speed, and the direction you're going. From this information, you can estimate or deduce your position. In fact, to help you remember what dead reckoning is, think of *dead*—or *ded*—as short for *deduced* (which is possibly how the phrase *dead reckoning* originated).

Determining your dead reckoned position from within a kayak is a little more difficult. Let's say you're paddling your kayak from Oldport to Newport. Whereas the previous example took place on a road (which severely limited the amount of wandering you could do), your travel within a kayak isn't limited to a narrow corridor between yellow and white painted lines. Therefore, dead reckoning in this example will require the additional step of determining direction. Thankfully, your compass can give you quick and accurate answers. Let's say you've maintained a heading of 90° since leaving Oldport. Next, you'll need to determine your speed. Unfortunately, you won't have a speedometer in your cockpit, so you'll need to esti-

mate. Again, dead reckoning is at best an educated guess, so there's no need to obsess over your actual speed; besides, wind and currents can affect your speed and course. A kayaker is most likely traveling at an average speed of 3 or 4 knots. Next, check your watch. Let's say you've been paddling for a half hour. A half hour at roughly three knots means you will have traveled approximately 1.5 nautical miles. Last, you'll need to transfer this information to your chart. Use a pencil to draw a line in the direction of 090° magnetic from Oldport. Use the chart's scale to estimate how long you should draw your line to represent 1.5 nautical miles. The end of the line represents

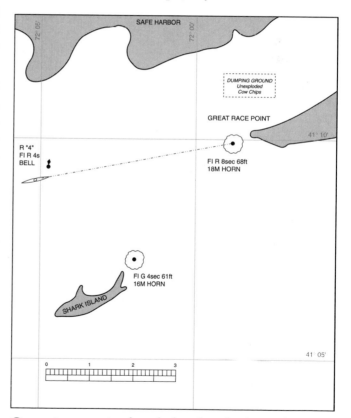

Comparing your view from the kayak to the chart to locate your position.

your dead reckoned position. (Don't worry if the process of transferring information to the chart sounds confusing; in the next chapter, we'll discuss how to use the chart's compass rose and how to accurately transfer distances to a chart using a pair of dividers.)

Kayak as Clock: An Alternative Method

Many times, you will not need to know your exact location; an approximation will do. And if you have enough clues, you won't even need a compass. Let's say you're traveling in the same waterway but further out this time. You're paddling in a northerly direction and you can see two lighthouses. Between the two lighthouses, and closer to the left one, is a small structure.

Now imagine your kayak as a clock, with the bow as 12 o'clock and the stern as 6 o'clock. From these reference points, one lighthouse is at 9 o'clock and the other at about 10:30, as shown in the illustration below.

Next, consider the facts and consult the chart to determine your approximate position. Here's what you know:

- You started your trip to the south of these lighthouses, so you know you're traveling north, which is toward the top of the chart. This confirms your direction.
- You know the two lighthouses are to your left with a land mass behind them. This places you somewhere to the east of the lighthouses.
- You see a buoy on the chart, which would be the small structure between the lighthouses.

Imagine your kayak as a clock: the bow is at 12 o'clock and the lighthouses at 9 o'clock and 10:30.

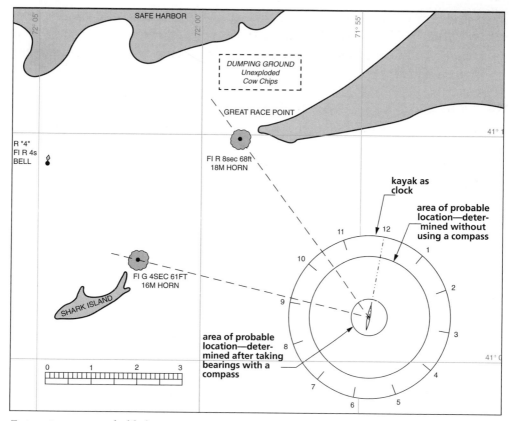

Estimating your probable location.

Knowing these facts, try to deduce a point on the chart from which the lighthouses would be at 9 o'clock and 10:30. To improve this estimate, be sure to also consider the location of the buoy. Although the area of uncertainty is quite large, at least you know you're still in the ballpark. If you had a compass with you, you could get a more accurate fix by taking bearings to both landmarks and plotting them on the chart (see Chapter 2). Your location would be the intersection of the two lines.

Definitions

I've already used the word *bearing* a few times, so at this point, I'd like to define the three fundamental names given to directions:

- Heading is the direction the kayak is pointed.
- Course is the direction you want to go.
- Bearing is the direction to a landmark.

These terms may seem very similar, but it's important to note their distinctions. As you can see in the illustration below, the compass values associated with each term are quite different. Let's say your destination is 90 degrees from your present location; to get there, you'll travel a *course* of 90 degrees. It's a blustery day, however, and you need to compensate for the wind in order to stay on the course line. Therefore, you adjust your *heading* to 120 degrees. Although it may appear you're paddling to some other destination, the persistent wind will keep you on the course line toward your objective. A *bearing* is a compass value that describes the position of an object relative to your present position. In the illustration, the lighthouse is at 50 degrees from your location. As we'll discuss in the next chapter, taking bearings on charted landmarks is a very useful when determining your location.

TRUE NORTH AND MAGNETIC NORTH

As everyone knows, the Earth spins on its axis—a conceptual line that runs through the center of the earth and terminates at the north and south poles. Maps and charts are usually aligned to the north pole; the top of a chart is oriented due north and all the chart's longitudinal lines eventually converge onto this single geographic point. This map orientation is known as *true north*.

Unfortunately, magnetic compasses do not point directly north; rather they point to *magnetic north*, which currently is located about 800 miles from the north pole, somewhere in the vicinity of Ellef Ringnes Island in the Queen Elizabeth Islands of Northern Canada. And, not only are magnetic north and true north not in the same location, but to make matters worse, magnetic north shifts slightly each year. Current findings are that the average position of the magnetic pole is moving at the rate of over 6 miles per year. To compound the confusion even further, solar winds can cause short-term and even daily shifts of up to 50 miles. Not to worry though. Because we are so far from magnetic north, the difference in the angle is quite small and doesn't affect us much.

Bearing, course, and heading.

It's not known for sure what causes the Earth's magnetic field. Modern theories hold that it is created by molten iron in the earth's outer core. Regardless of its cause, we as navigators must deal with it.

If you look at the photo on the following page, you will see two dark lines forming a V. The line on the right runs up a line of longitude to the north pole. The line on the left represents a compass pointing toward magnetic north. This V—the angle between true north and magnetic north—is called *variation*. (You may hear it referred to as *declination*, but that word is used more for on-land navigating, or *orienteering*. The way I remember that variation pertains to navigation on water is that the v in variation also appears in the word waves.) This information will come in handy later when we discuss the compass rose.

LATITUDE AND LONGITUDE

Imaginary lines called latitude and longitude form a grid around the Earth. These can be used to identify any geographical position on the Earth.

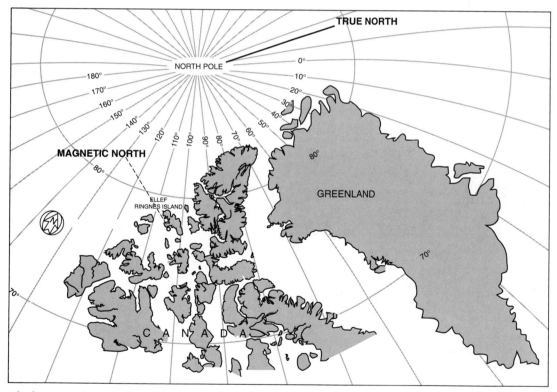

The location of magnetic north versus true north.

DECLINATION VS. DEVIATION

The words *declination* and *deviation* are both used in navigation and they can easily be confused. As noted earlier, *declination* is used when navigating on land and refers to the angular difference between true and magnetic north. Deviation is compass error that is caused by magnetic interference. Usually the source of interference is from nearby electronics or metal on the boat. Luckily, in most cases, a compass can be adjusted to compensate for errors.

In a kayak, deviation is not usually an issue. However, it is a good idea to be sure your compass is pointing where it should be. To check for deviation, compare the readings on your hand compass to your deck-mounted compass. They should match. If the compasses have different readings, first check that the handheld compass is not near a metal object, then look for something in the items you've packed that might be affecting the deck compass. Is the metal stove under the deck compass? Is an electronic instrument such as a weather radio or a GPS receiver too close? Relocating the offending object should correct the deviation.

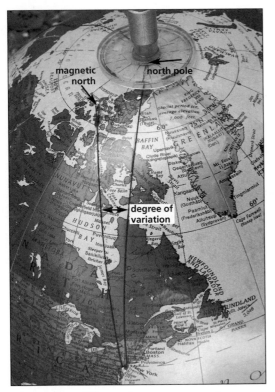

The angular difference between true and magnetic north is called the variation.

Longitude

As we discussed earlier, longitude lines run vertically, intersecting at the north and south poles (similar to the sections of a peeled orange). Longitude lines are also called *meridians of longitude*, or simply *meridians*.

Latitude lines run horizontally east to west. Unlike lines of longitude, lines of latitude never intersect one another. For this reason, they are also known as *parallels of latitude*, or *parallels*.

Lines of longitude and latitude are both measured in degrees. Each degree (°) is further divided into 60 minutes (′), and each minute into 60 seconds (″), similar to a clock. By using all three units, we can more precisely identify a position.

But first we need a starting point. Where do we begin measuring the degrees, minutes, and seconds? Where is zero?

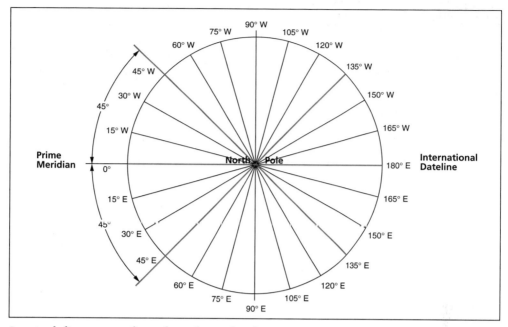

Longitude lines as seen from above the north pole.

For longitude lines, zero degrees is at the *prime meridian*—the imaginary north–south line that runs through Greenwich, England.

Let's imagine for a moment that you're standing on the ice directly above the north pole. Stretch your arms out in front of you, press both hands together, and point toward Greenwich. In this instance, both hands are pointing at zero degrees. Next, keep your left hand pointed in the same direction, but move your right hand such that you're pointing slightly west of Greenwich; stop when your arms are separated by a one-degree angle. That one-degree angle means that your right hand is now pointing down the 1° W meridian. Now, continue moving your right arm westward. Each time the angle between your arms increases by one degree, you'll be pointing down a new meridian. For instance, if there's a forty-five-degree spread between your arms, your right hand will be pointing down the 45° W meridian. If you continue spreading your arms until your right arm is as far away from the left as possible, the angle between your arms will be 180 degrees, and your right hand will be pointing down the international dateline, or the 180° meridian.

If you were to perform the same exercise but you instead kept your *right* hand pointed at Greenwich, then your left hand would point at eastern meridians. In other words, all meridians to the west of Greenwich are designated west, or W, and all meridians east of Greenwich are designated east, or E.

Latitude

For lines of latitude, zero degrees begins at the equator—the imaginary east–west line that circles earth's astronomical midpoint. Lines of latitude are measured a bit differently from lines of longitude.

To show you the difference, let's revisit the previous example, only this time we'll imagine ourselves at the earth's core. From your cozy little spot at the center of the earth, stretch your arms out in front of you, press both hands together, and point toward the equator at the distant surface of the earth. Both hands are pointing at zero degrees. Next, move your right arm northward slightly until your arms are spread apart by one degree. Your right arm will be pointing toward a point on the earth's surface that is *intersected* by the 1° N parallel, it will not be pointing *along* the parallel. To further illustrate this point, keep your arms locked in their current position, and pivot all the way around on your feet. As your body turns, your left hand will trace along equator, while your right hand will trace along 1° N.

Do you see how parallels are measured differently from meridians? Take a look at the illustrations if it's still a little hazy.

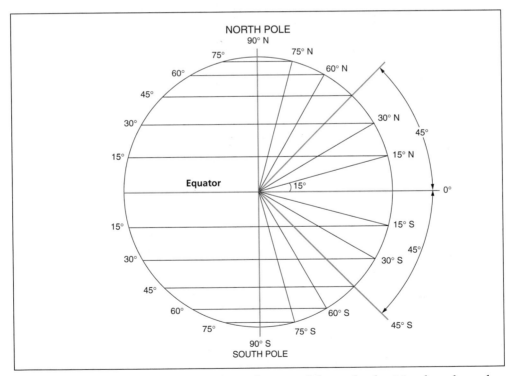

Latitude lines run horizontally east to west and are parallel to each other. Note how the angle of each parallel is measured from the earth's core.

A MILE A MINUTE

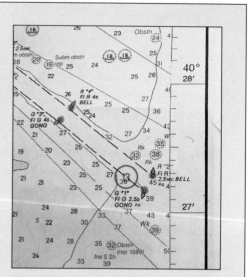

Why is it important to understand that longitude and latitude are measured differently? Well, let's start with a seemingly unrelated fact:

One degree of latitude is equal to 60 nautical miles. Therefore, if a minute of latitude is ¹⁄₆₀th of a degree, then *one minute of latitude equals one nautical mile*. This fact can be pretty handy while plotting on paper charts. For instance, if your chart is folded in a manner that you cannot see the scale, you can use the latitude lines on the chart's margins.

Latitude lines are parallel to one another so, no matter where you are, this equivalency holds true. Longitudinal lines, on the other hand, are not parallel; they get closer and closer to one another as they approach the poles. Therefore, one minute of longitude will only equal one nautical mile *if you're at the equator.*

The right- and left-hand margins of a chart can be used as a scale. Each minute of latitude equals one nautical mile, so you could use the space between 27′ and 28′ to help determine distances.

There are a total of 180 degree lines describing latitude. The latitude at the north pole is 90° N and the latitude at the south pole is 90° S. Parallels north of the equator are given the N designation, and parallels south of the equator are designated S.

Determining Coordinates (LatLon)

We can use parallels and meridians—and their associated minutes and seconds—to describe any location on the face of the earth. When describing a position, latitude is always given first, longitude second (LatLon). One example is 39° 38.05′ N, 074° 28.7′ W, which is the location of my house in New Gretna, New Jersey. We'll discuss how to do this in Chapter 9.

CHARTS

A nautical chart depicts a portion of the Earth's surface in a scaled drawing. Charts differ from maps in that they show details such as water depths, tidal ranges, shoreline composition, buoys, lights, and other things of interest to mariners. Charts

HOW USEFUL ARE IMAGINARY LINES?

- We can communicate an exact position to anyone. If you paddle familiar areas, you'll generally have little need to know your LatLon since it may be better to describe your position relative to a conspicuous landmark. However, an incident may arise that may necessitate informing someone of your location who is not familiar with the landmarks. Then it would be wise to give LatLon.

- If you are out-of-sight of discernable landmarks and have a Global Positioning System (GPS) receiver, the GPS will tell you the LatLon, and you can find your precise location on the chart. With a VHF radio, you could then inform someone of your whereabouts if the need arises.

- Every year the Coast Guard produces the Light List, a publication identifying the LatLon of every buoy, light, and federally maintained aid to navigation. If you have this publication and find yourself next to one of these aids, you can pinpoint your location. This list, along with chart lists from the National Oceanic and Atmospheric Administration (NOAA) and the Notice to Mariners, can be found on the Web.

- We can use latitude lines to determine distance on charts.

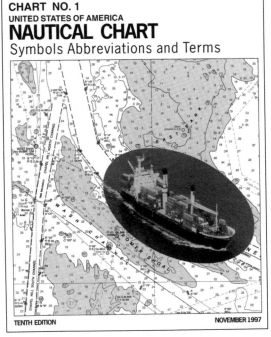

Chart No. 1.

employ many different symbols, terms, and abbreviations that may be unfamiliar to you. To learn them, pick up a copy of *Chart No. 1* or Nigel Calder's *How to Read a Nautical Chart* from a book store or chandlery. You can also download *Chart No. 1* from the internet (see Appendix B, Online Navigation Resources).

Compass Rose

Every nautical chart will have at least one compass rose printed on it. A compass rose will help you to orient yourself to north. Remember our earlier discussion on *variation*? As shown in the figure, an arrow on the compass rose points in the direction of true north and a separate arrow points to magnetic north;

the angle formed by these two arrows represents the amount of variation for that region. (In Chapter 2, you'll learn how to adjust for this variation when going from chart to compass or compass to chart. At the center of the compass rose the amount of local variation and the annual increase or decrease in variation is clearly printed. As a kayaker, you can ignore annual increases and decreases. This form of variation is measured in minutes—not degrees. Therefore, by the time the annual variation changes enough to affect navigation (i.e., 1 or 2 degrees), the chart will be long outdated. For example, with an annual increase of 4 minutes, it would

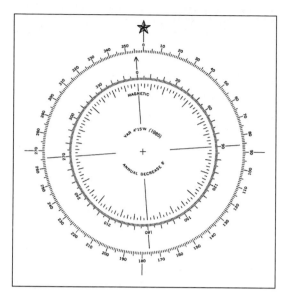

A typical compass rose.

take 15 years for the variation to shift by one degree (remember one degree equals sixty minutes). Besides, it is nearly impossible for a kayaker—in a tiny, wind- and wave-swept boat—to take bearings or follow a course line within a one- to two-degree margin of error.

Chart Scale

The scale of a chart is expressed as a ratio. If a 1:1 ratio indicates full size, then a 1:2 ratio is half the size, and so on, and so on. So, the larger the second number, the smaller the scale. Scale is important to a kayaker as it will determine the amount of detail the chart contains. For example, a 1:20,000 ratio is a larger, closer view than 1:40,000.

Seeing as how kayakers—a relatively slow-moving breed of mariners—don't travel great distances in a day, our needs are better served by a larger-scale map. Why? Because a very small-scale chart may omit many of the details we need to know—such as the location of underwater rocks. (I know what you're thinking: With such a shallow draft under our boats, is it really important for a kayaker to know these things? Well, large deep-water swells may suddenly be forced upward by an underwater rock and break explosively above it. Do you want to be paddling over said rock when this happens?) Also, the coastal profile will be less accurate on a small-scale chart, making it harder to tell if there is a suitable beach for landing or if the shore access is guarded by sharp rocks or tall cliffs.

A 1:40,000 scale is about the smallest scale a chart can go and still be useful for reading shoreline features. Let's break down the ratio: 1:40,000 means that 1 unit on the chart equals 40,000 units on the Earth's surface. Therefore, every inch on the chart equals 40,000 inches (or 3,333.33 feet or 0.56 nautical miles) in the real world.

A 1:20,000 scale chart of the same area would be more meaningful for our use. It would more clearly show the smaller coves where we might take shelter, and it would depict the shoreline composition, whether or not it is sand, rock, or mud. This information is highly useful. I prefer not to land on a mud beach if I have a choice.

Keep in mind, however, that with a 1:20,000 chart, the area covered will only be about 10 miles across. Taking large-scale charts on a long, multiday expedition means you'll need to carry a formidable stack of paper. If you have a long trip scheduled, use a small-scale chart for planning the overall route and consider carrying larger-scale charts for the areas you intend to land.

Waterproofing

NOAA charts are produced on paper, since they are made primarily for use on larger craft where they rarely get wet. When paper charts are used for kayak navigation, even if laminated or placed in a protective chart case, they eventually become soaked with water. Although charts can be waterproofed by applying a coat of water sealer (sold in most home supply stores), they should still be kept inside a map case. As an alternative, several aftermarket companies reproduce waterproof versions of NOAA charts. Although initially more expensive, waterproof charts are worth the extra cost and may eventually pay for themselves. You can buy them at the same boating store that sells marine supplies.

Topographical Maps

Other useful navigation tools for kayakers are topographic maps from the U.S. Geological Survey (USGS) and county maps. These are great to use when poking around the shore, rivers, or creeks. They are at a larger scale and tend to show accurate depictions of little creeks and marshes. Without them, especially in the marshes, it is quite easy to get lost. From the low perspective of a kayak, all low-lying sedges look the same.

The National Oceanic and Atmospheric Administration (NOAA) produces most American charts. Free pamphlets list the available charts for different regions; you can obtain these pamphlets and charts at any store that sells marine supplies.

Chart in waterproof case. The D-rings at the corners can be used to secure the chart to the deck lines.

AIDS TO NAVIGATION

Lights

There are three main types of lights in coastal navigation:

1. **Primary seacoast lights.** These are the lighthouses. They are conspicuous, stationary structures, each with a very powerful beam of light that can be seen for 15 to 25 miles, and they help navigators make their way along the coast or guide them towards land or a harbor entrance. The light—usually a white light—is displayed as flashing or as groups of flashes. For lighthouses located close together, the flashing patterns differ to avoid confusion at night. And to avoid confusion in the daytime, each lighthouse is uniquely constructed and painted.

2. **Secondary lights.** Less powerful than primary seacoast lights, secondary lights can generally be seen for 2 to 5 miles, and they help guide boats into harbor or river entrances, or other waterways. These lights can be white, green, or red.

3. Minor lights. These low-intensity lights can generally be seen for up to 2 miles, and they help guide boats through channels or around hazards such as shoals. These lights are generally white, green, or red. Lighted buoys also fall into this category.

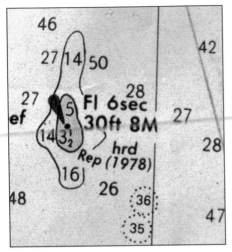

The light symbol on this chart indicates a flashing light (Fl) every 6 seconds (6sec), 30 feet above chart datum (30ft), that can be seen for 8 miles (8M) in clear weather.

Lights on Charts: Understanding the Notations

Charts have specific labels associated with light symbols. One example is *Fl 6sec 30 ft 8M* (see illustration). This notation indicates the presence of a light that flashes every 6 seconds, it has been mounted 30 feet above the sounding datum (usually the mean lowest low water), and it can be seen from a distance of 8 miles in clear weather. Again, you can learn more about symbols in *Chart No. 1.*

DIFFERENT TYPES OF LIGHTS

A flashing light (Fl) is just one of a few navigation lights you may experience while on the water. So what are the other kinds of lights and how does one tell them apart? The table below will give you an idea.

TYPE OF LIGHT	ABBREVIATION	DESCRIPTION	PATTERN
Fixed	f	Emits a constant beam of light	LLLLIIIIGGGGHHHHTTTT
Flashing	Fl	Total duration of light is shorter than total duration of darkness	Light Light Light
Isophase	Iso	Duration of light and darkness are of equal length	Light Light Light Light
Occulting	Oc, Occ	Total duration of light is longer than the total duration of darkness	Light Light Light Light Light Light
There are many other light characteristics covering coastal, intracoastal, and inland waters, the details of which are covered in the U.S. Coast Guard's publication called *Light List.*			

In general, a navigation light located in an area where background lights are present (such as streetlights, dock lighting, or house lights) will not be a fixed-beam type. In these instances, navigation lights must have characteristics that distinguish themselves from background lights.

Distance

The range or distance from which the light can be seen is listed next to the symbol on the chart. The printed distance assumes that the observer is peering at the light from a height of 15 feet above sea level—in other words, it is assumed that you'll be aboard a fairly large vessel. A kayak, however, is not a large vessel. Sitting in our cockpits, our eyes are only about 30 inches above the water, roughly 13 feet below the assumed value. Therefore, even on a clear day, a light that is purported to be visible at 8 miles will be out of range. Thanks to the curvature of the earth, the light will be behind the horizon, from our vantage point (see illustration on following page). In order to see the light, we'll need to paddle much closer.

Buoys and Markers

The main purpose of aids to navigation, or *atons*, such as buoys, beacons, and markers is to keep boats from straying into shallow water. Red atons will mark one side of the channel and green atons mark the other; boaters who stay between these red and green buoys, generally stay out of trouble. In U.S. and Canadian waters, buoys are arranged to follow this simple rule: *Red Right Returning*. This means that

LEFT: *Most lighthouses are located in conspicuous places, such as a headland, an offshore island, or a noticeable place along a cliff. This one is in Anglesey, Wales.* RIGHT: *Other lighthouses may mark shoals, breakwaters, or low-profile points of land such as this lighthouse in Bras d'Or Lake in Nova Scotia.*

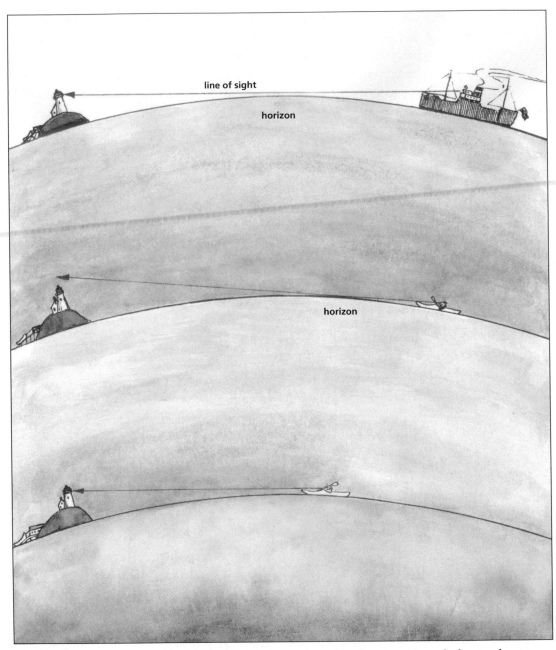

The curvature of the earth affects our ability to see objects at great distances. From the low-angle vantage point of a kayak, however, the distance at which we can see objects is substantially shortened. Notice how much closer the horizon is to the kayaker than the larger boat? It's important to note that the distances at which lights are purported to be visible were calculated with larger boats in mind.

mariners returning home from the sea can expect to see red buoys on the right side of the channel as they enter harbors or marinas. This rule doesn't always work, however. For instance, when you're traveling on the Atlantic Intracoastal Waterway, there's no clear cut way to define which way is "returning." In ambiguous cases like this, it helps to picture the United States as though it were a clock face. Boaters who are traveling in a clockwise direction along the U.S. coast will find the red buoys on the right-hand side.

Larger channels may have mid-channel markers which function like a road's yellow centerline.

Buoys

Buoys come in different shapes and colors; each one is labeled with a number. Just as navigation lights are available in a range of different flashing patterns, some buoys are equipped to emit a particular sound.

A buoy can have one of four sound signals: bell, gong, whistle, or horn:

- A bell buoy has one tone. As wave action rocks the buoy, one of four clappers strikes the bell.
- A gong buoy has four different tones. Four gongs are stacked vertically on the buoy, each with its own clapper.
- Whistle buoys (abbreviated as WHIS on charts) are operated by air compressed by wave action and are generally found in deep waters.
- Horn buoys are powered by batteries.

Buoys with sound signals are usually lighted as well.

The shape of a buoy can be significant; a buoy's shape often corresponds to its color. Green buoys, for instance, are often cylindrical in shape and, for this reason, have earned the nickname *can* buoys. Red buoys are often conical in shape; these are known as *nun* buoys. Being able to differentiate between these two shapes can be helpful in low-light situations when a buoy's color is less apparent.

Typical can buoy.

21

PREDICT THE FUTURE

Excepting certain controlled areas, no rule dictates that large vessels must stay in the channel; however, most boaters will do so to eliminate any chance of running aground. Now that we understand how buoys are placed and who's likely to follow them, we may be able to predict the route of certain vessels and stay out of their way. A vessel entering near-shore waters will keep the red buoys to the right, or starboard, and keep the green to port. When heading out to sea, the boat will keep the green buoys to starboard. While large vessels often need to travel within the deep-water channels, a kayak—with its shallow draft—does not. This doesn't mean that you will always be out of harm's way if you stay outside of the channel. Many boats, especially pleasure craft, travel outside the channel. Be sure to keep your eyes open and pay attention to what's going on around you.

As a kayaker, it is wise to use the Bigger and Uglier Rule: if it's bigger and uglier than you, stay out of its way.

The numbering system on buoys is also significant. Green buoys are affixed with odd numbers, red buoys are even. There are other types of buoys, such as mooring, special purpose, and seasonal, each with different characteristics. Some have fog signals or radar reflectors.

If you would like to learn more about this topic, check out Chart No. 1, the publication mentioned earlier in this chapter, and view all the many symbols.

Typical lighted buoy.

BUOYS ON CHARTS: UNDERSTANDING THE NOTATIONS

Buoys are marked on charts with specific information, such as number or letter, color, light characteristic, and sound characteristic. An *R* next to the buoy indicates a red light, *G* a green light, and *Y* a yellow light. When no color abbreviation appears on a lighted buoy, it is assumed to be white.

Numbers or letters that are marked on a buoy are enclosed in quotation marks such as "4" or "B." Buoys are numbered in order with the numbers increasing in the returning direction.

Most charts mark latitude and longitude next to the buoy; others have a circled number

Buoy Characteristics

	GREEN BUOYS	RED BUOYS	RED-AND-WHITE BUOYS
Location	Generally kept to port when returning from sea	Generally kept to starboard when returning from sea	Generally located mid-channel
Shape	Cylindrical in shape (can); sometimes topped with square daymarks	Conical in shape (nun); sometimes topped with triangular daymarks	Various shapes
Numbering	Odd numbers that increase from sea toward land	Even numbers that increase from sea toward land	Letters, not numbers
Color of Light (When Applicable)	Green lights	Red lights	White lights

LEFT: This state-placed buoy marks a dangerous sandbar. It also doubles as a convenient bird perch.
RIGHT: Solar-powered light on an intracoastal waterway daymark.

that corresponds to a table, located elsewhere on the chart, which contains coordinate information.

It's important to note that chart information is only accurate to the day it was published. Occasionally the coast guard will move, add, or remove buoys, or strong currents and winds might drag a buoy away from its charted location. This is why it's a good idea to purchase new charts frequently. In the meantime, any known

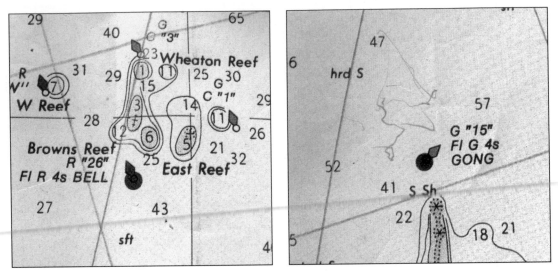

LEFT: *R "26," of Browns Reef, is a red bell buoy that flashes a red light every 4 seconds.* RIGHT: *G "15" is a green gong buoy that flashes a green light every 4 seconds.*

changes to charted buoys will be noted in the USCG publication *Notice to Mariners.* Also note that buoys that are not maintained by the USCG (state buoys, private, etc.) may not appear on charts at all.

Markers

You may find privately maintained channel markers dotting the edge of a channel to a local marina or other small waterway. Usually these markers are just painted wooden shapes mounted high on a pole that's been stuck in the seabed. Most of markers have no numbers. Double markers indicate the start of the channel.

LEFT: *Privately maintained red triangle channel marker.* RIGHT: *Privately maintained green square channel marker.*

LEFT: *Private red triangle double marker indicating the start of a channel.* RIGHT: *Private green square double marker indicating the start of a channel.*

NAVIGATION AIDS: AN OVERVIEW

There are many tools you can use to navigate. Some are used to do the actual navigating, others are for convenience, and some are for safety. Here's a list of essentials:

- Waterproof chart of area you will be paddling
- Hand compass
- Marine compass
- Waterproof tablet for taking notes
- Waterproof pen (writes underwater and even upside down)
- VHF Radio to monitor weather, boat traffic, or to use in an emergency
- Binoculars for seeing far off landmarks or buoy numbers
- Plotting tool (such as parallel rules) for course plotting

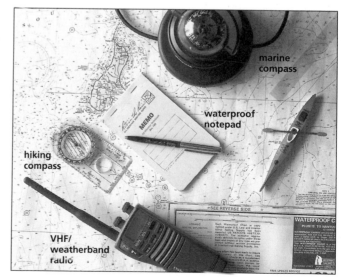

Essential navigation tools.

- Dividers for determining distances on charts, or a plastic grid (see Chapter 9)
- Scale-measuring instrument (to roll along an irregular route to get the distance)
- Local tide/current book

I will discuss most of these tools throughout this book, starting with one of the most important tools—the compass.

2 Using the Compass

EVELOPED ROUGHLY SEVEN CENTURIES AGO, THE simple magnetic compass is still an indispensable tool to the navigator. There are two types of compasses commonly used in kayak navigation: the marine compass and the handheld hiking compass (also called an orienteering or hand compass). Each compass has its own unique characteristics and purposes.

HIKING COMPASS

A hiking compass consists of three basic parts: the needle, the bezel, and the base plate.

The magnetic needle is stationary. No matter which way you turn the compass, the red end of the needle (the dark end in the photograph) constantly points north. The bezel, or compass dial, is imprinted with hatch marks around its perimeter (usually in two-degree increments) and orienting lines and an orienting arrow on its face. The bezel rotates atop the base plate. We'll discuss how to use the hiking compass in greater detail below, but for now you must know that in order to read the compass, the bezel needs to be rotated such that the orienting arrow is aligned under the red end of the needle. When you use a compass to take a bearing from a chart, you are actually using the compass as a protractor. The base plate may additionally have a ruler along the sides and the front or distance scales. (If it does have distance scales, they are calibrated to land miles, not nautical miles; however, you can add your own nautical scale with a waterproof marker.) Again, we'll discuss the nitty gritty later.

Handheld compasses have their own unique applications. For example, it is far easier to take a bearing to a landmark by aiming a hiker's compass than turning your

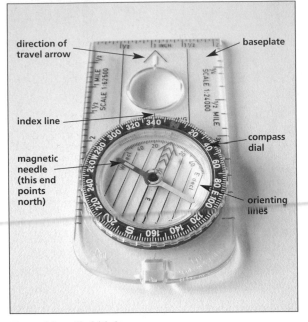

direction of travel arrow

baseplate

index line

compass dial

magnetic needle (this end points north)

orienting lines

Typical handheld hiking compass.

kayak around to face the object (as you'll see below). You can also take bearings from charts when plotting your course. Secure a hiker's compass to your personal floatation device (PFD) or to your deck line with a lanyard to keep from losing it. If you use string, you can mark it as a scale.

MARINE COMPASS

Marine compasses are mounted directly in front of the cockpit. Unlike a hiking compass, the needle in a marine compass is attached to a disk or ball. This disk—called a *compass card*—is imprinted with hatch marks and numbers; it sits suspended in clear liquid encased within a glass or plastic bubble. As the boat turns, the card remains stationary (relative to the Earth) while its casing turns smoothly around it. The liquid has a damping effect on the compass card; it eliminates any friction between the card and the casing, but it also serves as a shock absorber so the compass card gives a steady reading in choppy water. Imprinted on the face of the bubble is a hatch mark known as a *lubber line*. When installing a deck compass, the lubber line must be in line with the centerline of the kayak.

Using a marine compass is easy; whatever number lies directly behind the lubber line indicates the direction the bow is pointed.

There are permanently mounted compasses and portable ones. The portable marine compass has elastic cords that connect to your kayak deck lines.

The location of a deck compass is important. Most kayak manufacturers place the recess for the compass near the front hatch. If you're anything like me, you won't be able to see a compass in that location very well. I prefer to have my compass mounted on the front deck (allowing enough room to pull another kayak over the deck in the event of a rescue).

It's important to avoid placing any metal objects or electronic gizmos near the compass, as these items will cause false compass readings (i.e., deviation). Also, before you start out, it is wise to check your hand compass against the deck compass to be sure they agree.

LEFT: *A deck-mounted marine compass. In this example, the bow is pointed at roughly 195°.*
RIGHT: *A portable-style marine compass.*

COMPASS ROSE

Unlike hiking or marine compasses, a compass rose is a stationary, non-mechanical compass that is printed on all nautical charts. A compass rose consists of two rings: the outer ring relates to true north and the inner ring relates to magnetic north. As mentioned in the previous chapter, you'll also find information about the variation between true north and magnetic north at the center of a compass rose.

Adjusting for Variation

Adding or Subtracting

As navigators, the amount and direction of variation is what concerns us the most. Let's say you

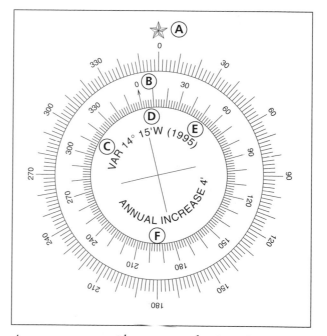

A compass rose provides a true north orientation on its outer ring (A), magnetic north orientation on its inner ring (B), variation (C), the direction of variation (D), the year the variation was measured (E), and the amount of annual increase (F).

29

want to paddle from Oldport to Newport. According to the chart, you'll need to travel a course of 090° T (true). Unfortunately, your deck-mounted compass provides readings in magnetic. If you were to paddle at a heading of 090° M, you'd miss your mark. How do we solve this situation?

Take a look at the compass rose featured in the illustration. We can see that the variation is 14° 15′ W. This means that there's a 14-degree discrepancy between true north and magnetic north. In order to determine the magnetic course to Newport, we'll need to either add or subtract 14° 15′ from 90°.

How do we know whether to add or subtract?

Well, there are two simple memory joggers that apply to adjusting variation from chart to field: "East is least, west is best" and "*POW* (plus on west)." In other words, if the variation is west, add it; if the variation is east, subtract it. So, in the above example, we'd add 14°* to 90°. To get to Newport from Oldport, we'd steer a course of 104° M (magnetic).

You can perhaps understand this better if you look at the compass rose: notice how magnetic north is west (left) of true north—in this case, about 14 degrees west of it.

Let's look at some more examples.

Example 1: The variation shown on your chart's compass rose is 15° W. You've plotted your course on the chart at 150 degrees, based on true north. You now have to see what heading to paddle. Since the variation is west, use *POW*! Add 15 degrees to 150 degrees, and paddle at 165 degrees. (Remember, this mnemonic device only works when you're adjusting variation from chart to field. If you're adjusting from field to chart [i.e., you take a field bearing and need to find it on your chart] do the opposite and *subtract* the variation.)

Example 2: The variation on your chart is 5° E. The course you plotted is 240 degrees. Since the variation is east, use "east is least" and subtract 5 degrees from 240 degrees and paddle at 235° M.

Techniques for the Math-Challenged

There's another way to adjust for variation; one that relies on tools rather than arithmetic. Be advised that this method works much better when sitting at the kitchen table than in a cockpit, so be sure to do your plotting ahead of time.

The first step is to spread out your chart and plot your course lines. Next, you'll

---

* As mentioned in Chapter 1, it's OK to drop the minutes or round up, when adjusting for variation, and it's OK to ignore the annual increases or decreases. All told, it might add or subtract one degree from your course line. It would be impossible to steer a kayak to that degree of accuracy. (No pun intended.)

need to employ a plotting tool. Two popular choices are a called a *plotter* and *parallel rules*. These tools are very easy to understand and use, but difficult to explain. Let's just say that these tools can be moved from one point on the chart to any other point of your choosing, and yet the tool's orientation to true north will remain unchanged. (Take a look at the illustrations and you'll immediately know what I'm talking about.) Align one of these tools to your course line. Next, move the edge of the plotter or parallel rules to intersect the very center of the compass rose. Not only will the edge of the tool intersect the center of the rose, but it will also intersect the inner and outer rings of the compass and thus present both the true and magnetic angles for your course line.

Let's turn to the accompanying illustrations. Let's say that Point A represents our put-in, and Point B is our destination. To plot a course:

1. Draw a straight line, in pencil, from the starting point (A) to the destination (B).
2. Line up a parallel tool on the course you've selected.
3. Walk or roll your parallel tool over until it crosses through the center of the compass rose.
4. Read the magnetic scale.

In this example, the reading shows 32 degrees magnetic. When jotting down a course or bearing, it is common to write *M* after the number to indicate magnetic, such as 032°M. If the number has no letter after it, it indicates a true course.

Next we determine the distance from Point A to Point B, either by using the scale on the bottom of the chart or the latitude lines along the right edge of the chart. We measure

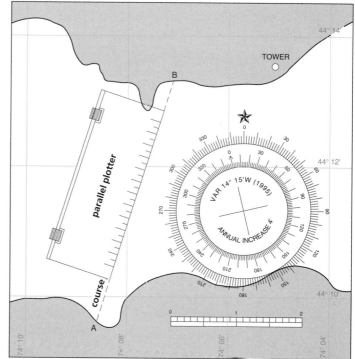

Line up a plotting tool on your course.

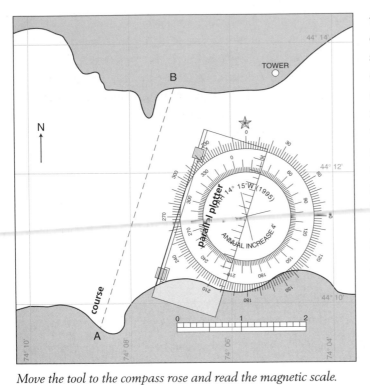

Move the tool to the compass rose and read the magnetic scale.

the distance by using a pair of dividers, a length of string, a piece of paper, or even our fingers. Our course measures about 3.9 nautical miles. How long will it take? If we assume our paddling speed to be, say, 3 knots (3 nautical miles per hour), it should take us approximately 1.3 hours (3.9 divided by 3). Simple—right? (Come on, put away that calculator.)

USING A HIKING COMPASS ON A CHART

A hiking compass is a versatile tool. Not only does its magnetic needle point help orient you in the real world, but it can also be used to help you interpret a printed chart.

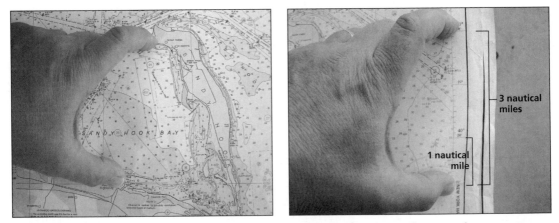

LEFT: Measuring distance from the put-in to the end of Sandy Hook. RIGHT: Place your fingers against the latitude lines. You can see that the distance for this trip is approximately 3 nautical miles, starting at 25 minutes and ending at 28 minutes.

Taking Bearings from a Chart

Now let's make the exercise a bit more challenging. Let's say that while we were packing for our trip we decided that—rather than bring a large chart—we'd photocopy only the portion of the chart that covers the area of our excursion. The narrow scope of our photocopy, however, didn't include the scale or a compass rose. Before leaving home, we added handwritten notes to the chart that indicate the variation and degrees of any available latitude and longitude lines.

If we don't have a compass rose, we won't be able to use a parallel tool to determine courses or bearings. Instead, we'll use a hiking compass as a stand-in for a compass rose. Start by placing one edge of the compass alongside the course line (see the illustration below), with the direction of travel arrow pointing the way we wish to go. Next we rotate the bezel, so that the orienting arrow is pointing in the same direction as chart north, and the orienting lines on the compass are parallel with the longitude (north/south) lines on our chart, or as close as we can get by eye (see illustration on next page).

Read the number of degrees on the compass dial that falls next to the index line. You should see a reading of about 18° for our exercise. To go from a chart bearing to a magnetic bearing, we must now add the variation: 18° (compass) plus 15° (variation) gives us 033°M.

To find the distance, fold a piece of paper into convenient units of one- or two-mile increments and measure it against the course line. You can also use the side of the compass: place one corner next to the zero end of the scale (if one is visible on your chart), then either mark a convenient distance on the side of the compass with a marker or hold your finger in place as a measuring point. Again, you can even place your fingers along the course at point A and point B, then

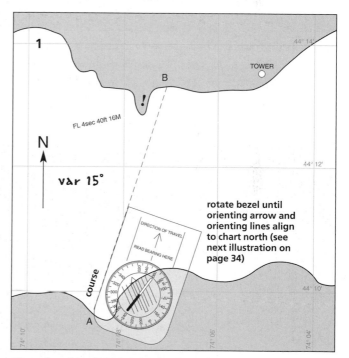

Place the edge of your compass along the course line, then rotate the bezel.

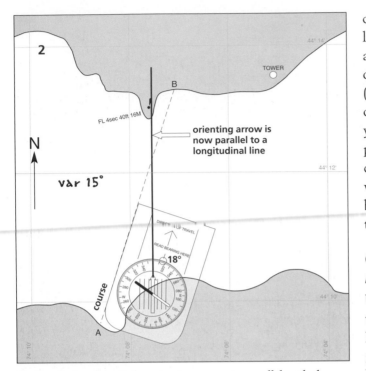

Rotate the bezel until the orienting arrow is parallel with the longitude line. Now you can take your bearing from the index line. (Note that the magnetic needle is irrelevant in this exercise.)

compare against the latitude lines. This will give an approximation of the trip distance as shown earlier. (You might also want to check how the width of your thumb or finger compares to the scale of your chart. For example, the width of two fingers might be about a half mile. Good to know.)

Getting a Fix on Your Location

Using a hiking compass to take bearings to real-life landmarks is a crucial navigation skill. Why? Taking bearings to charted objects will tell us exactly where we are.

Let's say that we're on our way from Oldport to Newport and we have been faithfully maintaining our predetermined compass heading. How do we know if the wind or current have carried us off course? If we can get bearings to at least two charted landmarks, we can get a *fix* on our location. (You may have noticed that during the previous exercise we did not use the magnetic needle of the compass at all—now we will.)

Taking Bearings to Landmarks

The first step is to find an object that you can see from the kayak that will also appear on the chart. Buoys, beacons, or lighthouses are perfect candidates, but you can also use land features such as islands, peninsulas, hilltops, and so on. Hold the compass so that the direction of travel arrow is pointed at the target (see illustrations on facing page).

Next, rotate the bezel so that the orienting arrow falls under the magnetic arrow. Read the bearing at the index line. For this exercise, it shows 7°.

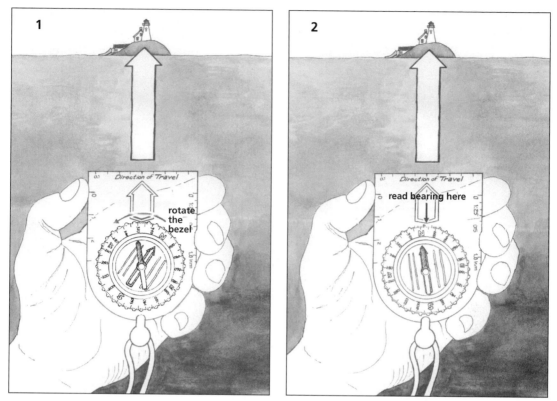

LEFT: Hold the compass so that the direction of travel arrow points at the target, then rotate the bezel. RIGHT: Rotate the bezel until the orienting arrow falls under the magnetic arrow. Read the bearing from the index line.

"Great," you say. "Now what?"

Well, next we'll have to apply that information to the chart.

Finding Where You Are on the Chart

First we need to convert our magnetic bearing of 007° M to a true reading. Let's say the variation for this region is 15° west. While the sayings "west is best" or "POW" tell us to add when converting chart numbers for the field, in this case we're converting field numbers to the chart, so we'll need to *subtract* the variation (7 − 15 = −8). The true north bearing, therefore, is 352° (360° − 8° = 352°).

Next, rotate the *bezel until* 352° aligns with *the index line.*

Place one of the upper corners of the compass on the chart symbol marking the lighthouse (see illustrations).

Pivot the compass around this point until the orienting lines within the bezel

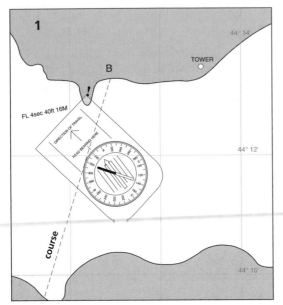

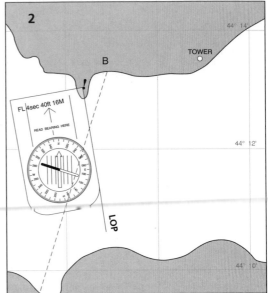

Rotate the bezel until 352° aligns with the index line. Then place one of the upper corners of the compass on the lighthouse symbol.

Pivot compass around the lighthouse symbol until the orienting lines align with the longitude lines and the orienting arrow points toward grid north. Use the compass edge to draw the LOP.

align with the longitude lines on the chart and the orienting arrow points towards grid north.

Now use the edge of the compass to draw a line from the lighthouse along the edge of the compass. We now know that we are located somewhere on this line (called a *line of position* or *LOP*), but we don't know exactly where.

To narrow the possibilities, we'll need to take a bearing to another charted object. Let's say this time we take a bearing to a water tower.

Perform the same exercise as you did with the lighthouse. The bearing to it is 053°M. Convert it to a true reading, by subtracting 15 degrees from 53 degrees, which gives you 038°M. *Set the compass to this bearing.* Place an upper corner of the compass on the symbol of the tower. Pivot the compass around this point until the orienting lines on the compass are parallel with the longitude lines on the chart and the orienting arrow points toward grid north. Draw a line from the tower along the edge of the compass. Extend the line if necessary until it crosses the first LOP. The intersection of these lines is very close to where you are. You have just fixed your position.

You'll notice that your position is approximately ½ nautical mile to the east

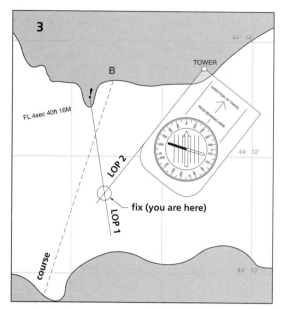

Set the bezel to 038° and place an upper corner of the compass on the symbol of the tower. Pivot the entire compass until the orienting lines and orienting arrow within the bezel are pointing to chart north. Draw a line from the tower along the edge of the compass. The intersection of this new line with the previous LOP will indicate your approximate position.

of your course line. Good thing you checked.

How to Navigate with a Hiking Compass

If you don't have a deck-mounted compass, you can navigate using a hiking compass, although it won't be as easy. First plot your course—we'll use 140°M—then rotate the bezel so that 140 lines up with the index (as in the photo on page 40).

Next set the compass flat on the kayak's foredeck or sprayskirt, with the direction of travel arrow pointing toward the bow of the boat. To travel in the correct direction, turn your boat until the magnetic needle aligns with the orienting arrow. Once these align, the bow will be pointing 140°.

Is Your Compass Facing the Right Way?

A common mistake when using a hiking compass for taking bearings from a chart is aligning the compass the wrong way (i.e., the direction of travel arrow is opposite to the direction you want to paddle). This results in a bearing that is 180 degrees off, known as a *reciprocal bearing*. There is a way to recognize what you are doing and to correct it, but it requires that you step back from the details and look at the larger picture.

Let's assume Janet and Joe are out kayaking, and fortunately for Joe, Janet has been paying attention to their surroundings. They are now at a point off the mainland. Looking at her chart, she sees that their final destination, a small island seven miles out, is northeast of where they are now. Even though they can't see the island, they prepare to paddle to it. Looking at the chart, Janet estimates their position by determining they are about 50 feet from the point and, for practice, asks Joe to plot a course.

YOUR INNER COMPASS

Some people have a great sense of direction; they are attuned to the earth's subtle clues, perhaps even without realizing it. Even if you don't have an innate sense of direction, there no reason why you can't develop better skills. As a kayaker, it's important to always have a general idea your direction, such as north, northeast, or east. Here are a few easy indicators to keep you oriented.

If it is late afternoon and the sun is to your left, you are facing north.

Each region provides its own clues. If you're paddling off the West Coast for example, you'll know you're traveling south if you see the mainland to your left.

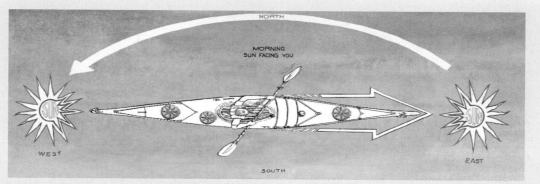

If it is morning and if the sun is facing you, you are facing east.

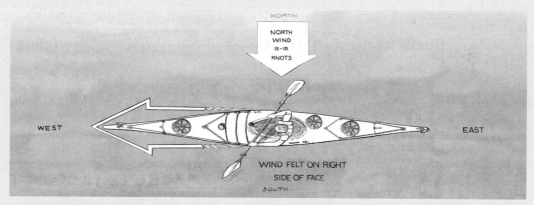

Memorizing weather forecasts can be helpful, too. If you know the day's weather calls for a north wind blowing at 12–15 knots, then you can reasonably estimate you're moving west if you feel strong wind on the right side of your face.

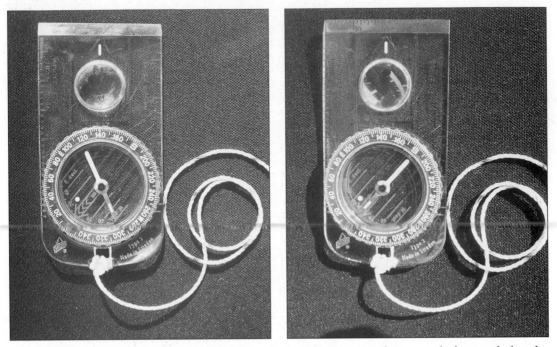

LEFT: First, rotate the bezel so that 140 lines up with the index. RIGHT: Then, steer the boat such that the magnetic needle aligns with the orienting arrow. You'll be steering a course heading of 140° M.

"I get 205 degrees to the island. Let's go!" Joe says.

"You're wrong—it's 25 degrees. Do it again." Janet replies.

"How can you be so sure? You didn't even watch me plot the course"

She draws a sketch similar to the one on the right.

"Well, Joe, from the chart, you can see that the island lies northeast of this point, which is also the direction we've been

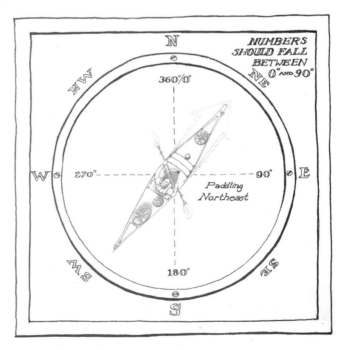

travelling. If you look at this sketch I just made, you can see that the bearing has to fall somewhere between 0 and 90 degrees. If we were heading south, the answer would be somewhere around 180 degrees."

"So if we want to go east, the bearing should be near 90 degrees. West would be about 270 degrees, and northwest would be between 270 and 360 degrees, right?"

"You're catching on" says Janet. "Now, let's stop talking and get paddling."

3 Tides and Tidal Currents

YOU MAY BE ASKING, "WHAT DO YOU MEAN BY TIDES and tidal currents? Aren't they the same?" The answer is no. It's important to distinguish between these two terms. Tides are the vertical motion of the ocean water rising and falling. A tidal current is the horizontal movement of the ocean.

First, let's define a few words we will be using in this chapter:

Flood tide. When water flows into a bay or estuary

Ebb tide. When water flows out of a bay or estuary

Slack water. When the water flow stops or is at its minimum. Occurs immediately after low and high tides, and lasts roughly 20 minutes

> *The way I see it, if you want the rainbow, you gotta put up with the rain.*
>
> DOLLY PARTON

WHAT CAUSES TIDES?

Tides are caused by the moon and, to a lesser extent, the sun. Although the sun is millions of times larger than the moon, it has a lesser effect because it's much further away. The gravity from the moon and sun pull the water up so that it starts to form a bulge. This bulge is the high tide. At the opposite end of the earth, another high-tide bulge forms due to centrifugal force. And, with so much water pulled toward the bulges, the ocean becomes shallower midway between the two bulges—these are the low tides.

During periods of full moons and new moons—when the moon and sun are in alignment with the Earth—the gravity of the two bodies combine to create a stronger pull, resulting in a higher high tide and a lower low tide. This phenomenon is referred to as a *spring tide*—no relation to the season.

Neap tides are not as extreme as spring tides. They occur when the moon is at a

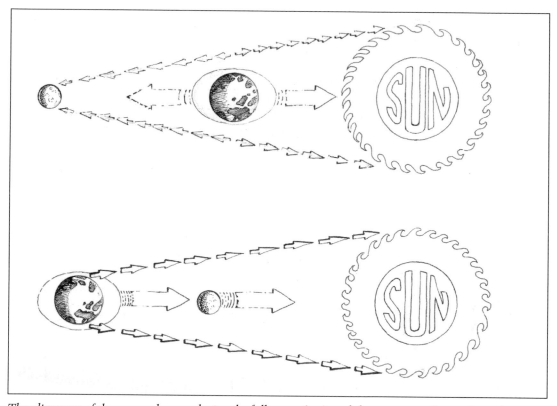

The alignment of the sun and moon during the full moon (top) and the new moon (bottom) results in a higher high tide and a lower low tide, called the spring tide.

90-degree angle to the Earth and sun, which is during the moon's first and last quarters. At this time, the gravity of the sun and moon pull in different directions so the tidal effect is minimized. The high tides will be lower, and the low tides will be higher than at spring tides.

The period between spring and neap tides is referred to as normal tides. The tide range is not as great as spring tides nor as little as neap.

All of this is made a bit more complicated by the fact that the moon is not in a circular orbit around the Earth but an elliptical one. When the moon is closest to the Earth, called perigee, the difference between high tide and low tide is greater than when the moon is the farthest from Earth (at apogee).

On the open ocean, the actual bulge height is only about 18 inches. It follows the moon, albeit there is some delay, and builds in height as it moves toward the shore, just as a wave does when it reaches shallower water. As it approaches land, where the sea floor starts to rise or the land gets constricted, the height of the tide

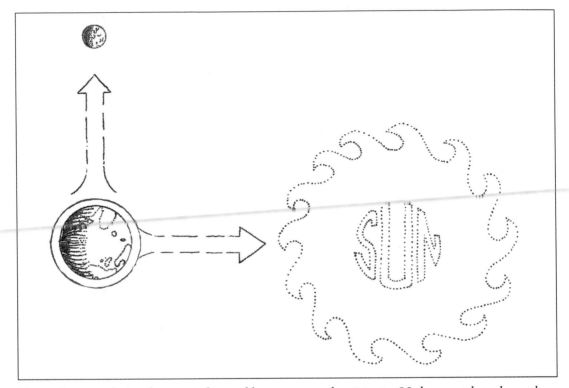

Neap tides occur during the moon's first and last quarters, when it is at a 90-degree angle to the earth and sun.

increases. In some areas, such as in the Bay of Fundy or the northern part of the Sea of Cortez, tides can reach exceptional heights of 40 feet.

It takes a while for the moon's gravity to overcome water's inertia, which is why the bulge lags behind the moon. The result is that the higher spring tide may lag an hour or two behind the meridian passage of the moon (i.e., when the moon is at its peak, crossing your longitude).

Tide cycles are diurnal, semidiurnal, or mixed, depending on the location. The word *diurnal* means daily, and in reference to tides, it means one high and one low tide per day. Very few areas have this type of tide cycle. A mixed cycle means two high tides and the two low tides daily, with a large difference in height.

Semidiurnal means there are two high tides and two low tides, of roughly the same height, occurring daily. Of the two cycles, one will have a higher tide than the other. We refer to the higher of the two as *higher high* and the other, the *lower high*. The same is true for the low tides. The higher of the two low tides is called the *higher low* and the other, the *lower low*. Usually, the difference is not great between the two cycles. These are known as normal tides: tides which take place between the spring and neap tides.

If the lower of the two normal high tides is 5 feet and the higher is 6 feet, there is an intermediate point between the two, 5 feet 6 inches, which is called mean high water (MHW). This is also true during spring and neap tides. We refer to the intermediate spring high tides as mean high water springs (MHWS) and the intermediate neap high tides as mean high water neaps (MHWN). Low tides are similar. There are mean low water springs (MLWS) and mean low water neaps (MLWN).

The tide cycles for most of the world, including the Atlantic coast, are semidiurnal with a time difference of about 6 hours and 15 minutes between high and low tides. Much of the Pacific coast has a mixed cycle, and the range between high and low of the second cycle can be much greater or much smaller than the first. It is actually possible for the higher low tide of one cycle to be higher than the lower high tide of the other cycle. (See, I told you, we would keep it simple.)

For those kayakers who paddle in areas with a small tidal range, knowing the times of the tides is not a high priority; however, for others, it can be very important. For example, understanding the tides might mean the difference between landing

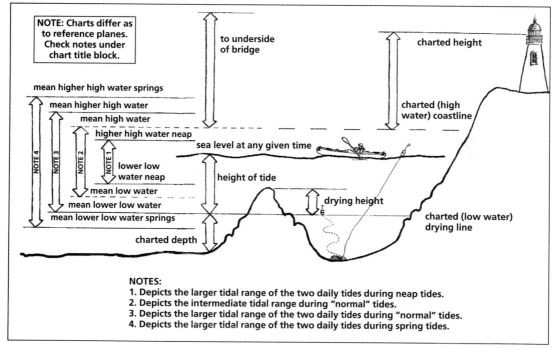

NOTES:
1. Depicts the larger tidal range of the two daily tides during neap tides.
2. Depicts the intermediate tidal range during "normal" tides.
3. Depicts the larger tidal range of the two daily tides during "normal" tides.
4. Depicts the larger tidal range of the two daily tides during spring tides.

The various tide heights.

on a nice beach at low tide or finding only rocks at high tide. Or in places where the bottom slopes very little, a low tide can be a mile or more from the high tide line. If you don't plan your trip well, including paying attention to the tides, you could end up dragging your kayak on a long, muddy walk back to solid land.

FINDING THE TIMES OF HIGH AND LOW TIDE

There are a number of ways to find the times of high and low tide. The marine forecast on the weather radio broadcasts the times of tides, and many newspapers list the times for various locations in its vicinity. The Internet is another source (see Appendix B, Online Navigation Resources), and computer software is now available that predicts tide times for almost anywhere in the country. Tide tables are available for free at many marine stores, or you can purchase the latest tide and pilot book, which, in addition to the tides, will have information on currents in certain areas, phases of the moon, as well as a plethora of other useful information.

Keep in mind that, just as with charts, these books are really made for larger vessels and rarely show current or tide data where we kayakers paddle. Sometimes we have to either interpolate or extrapolate the information for our use. Also keep in mind that these tables are predictions, and although usually quite accurate, they may differ from actual conditions due to weather, typographical errors, or errors in the government tables that are the informational source for these books.

Low tide, long walk: the bitter fruits of poor planning.

USING TIDE AND PILOT BOOKS

After perusing the tide and pilot book for your area and getting a feel for it, I suggest labeling sticky notes to tab the sections you will want to find quickly.

Tide tables use certain locations as reference points. Areas near these reference points state their high or low tides as so many hours and minutes, either before or after the time at the reference location. If, for example, Sandy Hook, New Jersey, had a high tide at 9:03 A.M. on a particular day, the tide table may state that high tide at Tom's River is 4 hours later, which would make it 1:03 P.M. Current tables are similar.

So, how do we use them? I'll give you an example, Since I live in New Jersey, I'll say our group will be doing a Christmas Day paddle, launching at 10:30 A.M. from the town of Tom's River.

First I turn to the section of my tide and pilot book that might be titled "Times of High Water" and find the area closest to where I am going to be paddling. The particular book I am using covers the area from Nova Scotia to Florida, arranged from north to south, which makes it easier to find a particular area. Looking in the book, I see a table similar to the one below. This table indicates that high water at the town of Tom's River is 4 hours after Sandy Hook.

Next I find the tide tables for Sandy Hook. Turning to the page for the month of December, I scan the row of information for the 25th (see table on following page). This tells me that morning high tide at Sandy Hook is at 2:33 A.M. and low tide is at 9:03 A.M.; the evening high tide is at 2:35 P.M. and low tide is at 9:11 P.M.

To each of these times, I add the difference of 4 hours and get the following at my launch site:

Times of High Water

NEW JERSEY COAST	HOUR–MINUTE		
Silver Bay	4–26	After	Sandy Hook
Coates Point	4	After	Sandy Hook
Tom's River	**4–00**	**After**	**Sandy Hook**
Seaside Park	3–40	After	Sandy Hook
Barnegat Inlet	0–12	Before	Sandy Hook

Tide Table for Sandy Hook						
DECEMBER						
	HIGH TIDE			**LOW TIDE**		
Day	Height	A.M.	P.M.	Height	A.M.	P.M.
24	4.0	1:46	1:42	3.8	7:59	8:20
25	**4.2**	**2:33**	**2:35**	**3.7**	**9:03**	**9:11**
26	4.4	3:23	3.34	3.7	9:59	10:00

High tide at (2:33 A.M. + 4:00 =) 6:33 A.M.

Low tide at (9:03 A.M. + 4:00 =) 1:03 P.M.

High tide at (2:35 P.M. + 4:00 =) 6:35 P.M.

Low tide at (9:11 A.M. + 4:00 =) 1:11 A.M.

From this information, I am able to determine that low tide will be at about 1:00 P.M., and if our group leaves at 2:00 P.M., the tide will have been rising for only one hour. If we knew the area to be very muddy at low tide, we would adjust our timing to leave about 4:30 P.M., so as to have a higher water level and (hopefully) less mud.

Although this was based on a book for my area, the tide and pilot books for other areas will be very similar.

RULE OF TWELFTHS

The rate at which the water level rises or falls with the tides is not constant, but it is predictable.

It takes about six hours for the water level to go from low tide to high tide, or vice versa. In the first and last hours of a tide change, the water rises or falls $1/12$ of its total range. In the second and fifth hours, it rises or falls $2/12$ of its range. And in the third and fourth hours, it rises or falls $3/12$.

This is known as the *Rule of Twelfths* (see table). If we divide the total amount of rise or fall into twelve equal parts, we can apply this handy principle.

To make it easier to understand, let's say you have a tidal range of 6 feet in your area. Let's also round the time difference between high and low tide from 6 hours and 15 minutes to 6 hours flat.

Rule of Twelfths			
TIME PERIOD	FRACTION OF TOTAL CHANGE	HEIGHT WATER LEVEL RISES IN THIS HOUR*	HEIGHT OF TIDE AT THE END OF THE HOUR*
1st hour	$1/12$	.5 ft	.5 ft
2nd hour	$2/12$	1 ft	1.5 ft
3rd hour	$3/12$	1.5 ft	3 ft
4th hour	$3/12$	1.5 ft	4.5 ft
5th hour	$2/12$	1 ft	5.5 ft
6th hour	$1/12$	.5 ft	6 ft
*This information is based on a region with a 6-foot tidal range.			

The first step is to divide the tidal range by 12. For our area (a 6-foot tidal range) each twelfth equals 0.5 feet. As you progress into the tide cycle, multiply 0.5 feet by the appropriate number of twelfths for the particular hour. Once you've determined the height change for that hour, add it to the sum of the previous hour(s). As you can see from the table and illustration on the following page, the water rises or falls slower in the first and last hours, and it rises or falls fastest in the middle two hours of the tide change. You can remember how these parts distribute themselves across the six-hour span by memorizing this saying: "1-2-3, 3-2-1."

CURRENTS

There are river currents as well as ocean or tidal currents. River currents flow in one direction, from a higher elevation to a lower one, while tidal currents are caused by the rising and falling of the tide. Thus tidal currents reverse direction. For example, when the tide is falling, the water moves horizontally trying to correct the imbalance of higher water at the coast and lower water in the bay. The reverse occurs when the water at the coast is lower. This horizontal movement is the tidal current. When it flows into an estuary, it is a flood current, and as it goes out, it is an ebb current. These currents are the ones that primarily concern kayakers. Other ocean currents are caused not only by the tide rising, but by surface winds, the revolution of the earth, and changes in water temperature.

You will hear the terms *set* and *drift* when referring to a current. *Set* is the direction the current is flowing to. A westerly set, therefore, means the current is flowing

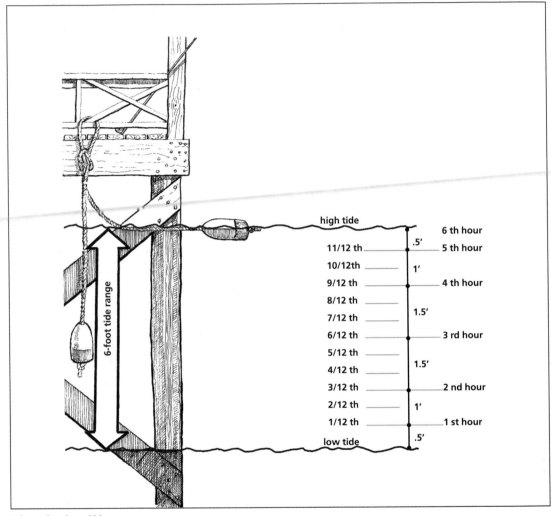

The rule of twelfths.

from east to west. In other words, as a kayaker riding this current, you are being set, or moved, to the west. *Drift* is the current's speed, in knots.

Depending on your destination, a current, like wind, can be your best friend or your worst nightmare; it can work to your advantage or it can fight against you.

The relationship between tide height and the tidal current is not always as you would guess. It seems reasonable to assume that when the tide stops going up or down, the current would stop. This reasoning is frequently wrong, and it can get a kayaker into serious trouble, especially with a strong current. It is actually possible for the tide to be rising and the current ebbing. Let's take a look at the accompanying illustration. Two glass vessels are connected by a small tube. The one on the right depicts the ocean, and the one on the left is a bay or estuary. The narrow tube is a constriction in the underwater topography between the two—perhaps a narrow channel or a shoal separating two deeper areas.

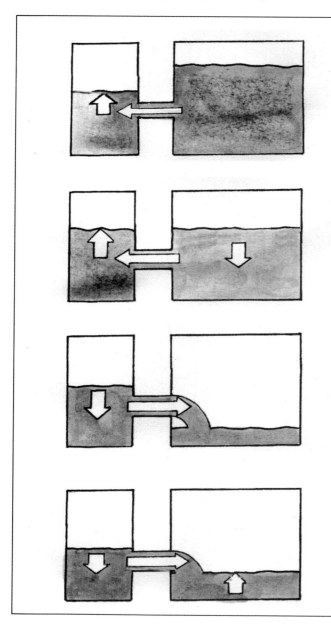

1. *The ocean at high tide. The water filling into the estuary cannot get through the opening fast enough. Although the ocean is at slack water for perhaps 15–20 minutes, the current is still flooding since the elevation of the ocean is higher.*

2. *The ocean is starting to fall but, because it's still higher than the estuary, it continues to flood the estuary until both bodies level out.*

3. *The ocean at low tide. The water continues ebbing from the estuary because the estuary is higher.*

4. *The ocean has started to rise but the elevation in the estuary is still higher; therefore, water continues to trickle out.*

. . . THE KINDNESS OF STRANGERS

Information on tides and currents can be hard to come by. Sure, tide tables and current tables provide this information for many areas, but they often don't cover areas of light ship traffic or moderate currents. (Keep in mind that although a 2-knot current might seem fast to someone in a kayak, it is nothing to worry about for someone in a powered vessel and therefore isn't reported on tables.) If you cannot find printed information on a particular area, ask around. Striking up a conversation with a fellow paddler or local fisherman may provide invaluable local knowledge.

A SCENARIO: CROSSING THE RACE

Suppose you're planning to paddle from Orient Point, at the western tip of Long Island, New York, to Little Gull Island on October 26. To get to the island, you will have to cross Plum Gut, a narrow area where currents can be very fast and dangerous. To limit the danger, you'll need to do some planning.

First, in your tide and pilot book find the table showing the times of current change for the appropriate area (see table on facing page). You notice that both the flood and ebb at Plum Gut occur 1 hour and 10 minutes before the same conditions occur at an area called The Race, and the average ebb current is 4.4 knots. (This may be faster than you can paddle.)

Staying on track in a strong current.

Times of Current Change

LONG ISLAND SOUND (BASED ON THE RACE)

	TIME DIFFERENCES	MAXIMUM FLOOD		MAXIMUM EBB	
	FLOOD STARTS, EBB STARTS HOURS–MINUTES	TRUE DIRECTION	AVG MAX IN KNOTS	TRUE DIRECTION	AVG MAX IN KNOTS
Little Gull Island, 1 mile ENE of	-0 05	290	4.2	120	4.8
Plum Gut	**-1 10**	320	3.5	120	**4.4**
Little Gull Island, 0.9 mile NNE of	Flood +0 15, Ebb -2 30	255	1.8	040	2.9

Next refer to the current tables of The Race, Long Island Sound.

Current Table of The Race, L.I. Sound

OCTOBER

DAY	NORTHWEST FLOOD STARTS			SOUTHEAST EBB START		
	A.M.	P.M.	KNOTS	A.M.	P.M.	KNOTS
25	6 06	6 41	A.M. 3.8	12 01	12 17	P.M. 4.3
26	**6 51**	7 30	**A.M. 3.8**	12 47	**1 03**	**P.M. 4.3**
27	7 40	8 21	A.M. 3.7	1 36	1 52	P.M. 4.2

Note: Maximum flood is 2 hours and 45 minutes after flood starts, plus or minus 15 minutes. Maximum ebb is 3 hours and 25 minutes after ebb starts, plus or minus 15 minutes.

Checking the time that the flood starts at The Race, you see it is at 6:51 A.M., with the strongest predicted flow of 3.8 knots at peak velocity for this location. From the previous table, you know that flood at Plum Gut starts 1 hour and 10 minutes before it starts at The Race, which works out to 5:41 A.M.

Notice the note on the bottom of the current table that states: "Maximum flood 2 hours 45 minutes after flood starts, plus or minus 15 minutes"; and "Maximum ebb 3 hours 25 minutes after ebb starts, plus or minus 15 minutes." If the flood at Plum Gut starts at 5:41, and you factor in that the maximum flood is 2 hours 45 minutes after flood starts, you'll find that the strongest current of about 3.5 knots (see Times of Current Change) will be at 8:26 A.M. Not a good time to be out there.

The ebb current starts at 1:03 P.M. at The Race, which means that at Plum Gut, it would start at 11:53 A.M. (1:03 A.M. minus 1:10) and increase in speed to the average fastest ebb current of 4.3 knots, occurring about 2:38 P.M.—an even worse time to paddle. A wiser choice for you may be to select a time halfway between full flood (8:26 A.M.) and full ebb (2:38 P.M.). This would be about 11:30 A.M., just before the ebb starts. Fortunately, this is a very short crossing, so you should be across Plum Gut before the current has time to build to full force.

The current speeds as shown in current tables or charts are generally the fastest you will encounter at maximum flood or ebb. For all other times, you will have to interpolate. Use the 50/90 Rule as shown in the table below:

50/90 Rule

	HOUR AFTER SLACK (SEMI DIURNAL)						
	SLACK	1	2	3	4	5	6
Percent of maximum rate	0	50	90	100	90	50	0

Let's plug in our time and maximum rate in the following table. We will do it for the slack prior to the ebb. From the above discussion, we know the ebb will start about 11:30 A.M., and the maximum current is 4.3 knots. We plug in 11:30 under the slack box and 4.3 under the 100 percent box and work out the rest of the times and percentages.

50/90 rule exercise

	HOUR AFTER SLACK (SEMI DIURNAL)						
	SLACK	1	2	3	4	5	6
Time	**11:30**	12:30	1:30	2:30	3:30	4:30	5:30
Percent of maximum rate	0	50	90	**100**	90	50	0
Speed in knots	0	2.15	3.87	**4.3**	3.87	2.15	0

IT'S ALL IN YOUR POINT OF VIEW

Fast currents and tidal races can be either exciting or terrifying, depending on your point of view and level of experience. The two photos below show Penrhyn Mawr, a notorious tidal race in Anglesey, Wales.

Paddling out to the race, the calm before the storm.

Playing in the race as the flood comes in. The noise from tidal races can be heard for quite a distance on shore.

Paddling in a tidal race.

The photo above shows a tidal race on the way to Bardsey Island at the western tip of the Lleyn Peninsula in Wales. There is a rock called Carreg Ddu between the mainland and Bardsey. The tidal range is about 33 feet in this area. During mid-tide, the water rushing over the rock can be heard for miles on shore. This is an area where you need to know how to read charts and anticipate what will happen as the tide floods and ebbs.

Remember: all the estimated calculations and predictions are only that—predictions; they can vary quite a bit depending on many factors. A prudent navigator realizes this and uses the data as a guide only. Keep in mind that navigation is an art as well as a science.

4 Preparing to Paddle

THERE ARE A LOT OF THINGS A PERSON CAN DO TO MAKE his or her kayak trip enjoyable: good company, fair weather, and, most important, sound preparation. Planning your trip not only includes plotting your route on the chart, but also requires you to know how to estimate your speed, understand ranges, and decide what gear is appropriate.

Most navigation should be done at home where you have time, room, and reference materials. This is the time to plot your courses, and plan according to tides and currents. You can even do what I like to call *pre-navigation*: preparing your chart ahead of time to make life easier later when you're on the water (see Chapter 8).

As the time gets closer, you should frequently check the weather. Don't hesitate to postpone the trip if things are not looking right. An ideal trip will use these elements to your advantage:

- **Weather**. Naturally, if you have a choice, select a period of time where forecasts predict good weather.
- **Wind**. This is probably one of the biggest factors in making or breaking a trip. Check the wind forecast to get an idea how it will affect your paddling.
- **Tides**. Know what time high and low tides will be for the area in which you will be paddling.
- **Currents**. Check charts and current tables (if available). The charts may be easier to get than current tables. The best place to get information on currents is from local knowledge. Ask other kayakers or small boat fishermen who live in the area where you will be paddling.

> *In all things, success depends upon previous preparation, and without such preparation, there is sure to be failure.*
>
> CONFUCIUS

In addition to planning your trip around favorable conditions, be sure to take these important steps:

- **Plot your course on a chart.** With a pencil, lightly draw your course lines on the chart. Add magnetic bearings, distances, and even estimated times.
- **Trip table.** Rather than, or in addition to, plotting the above information on the chart, make a trip table like the one shown below. You can print it on waterproof paper or put it in a small plastic sandwich bag to prevent it from getting wet. A trip table should consist of bearing, distance, estimated time for each leg, and notes about the trip.

  To estimate time, you must first have a good idea of how fast you paddle. Paddling speed is the result of many factors, which we'll cover in more detail shortly. As a starting point use about 3 knots (3 nautical miles per hour), which is a fairly average speed. Remember that you may paddle at a different speed when traveling with a group.

- **Make a float plan.** The information on a float plan should include the items shown in the figure, plus anything that will help rescue teams locate you. Use as many sheets as you need. Leave your float plan with a responsible family member. The Coast Guard will usually not accept float plans; they have more important things to do than monitor your trip. If you fail to return at the time stipulated in the float plan, the person who has your float plan should contact the Coast Guard to give them the information.
- **Plan escape routes.** When planning your trip, always try to have an alternate plan to seek shelter or to get the group to safety if things go wrong.

Sample Trip Table

LEG NO.	MAGNETIC BEARING	DISTANCE (NM)	EST. TIME	REMARKS
1	050	1.5	30 min.	To Barren Island
2	080	.75	15 min.	To No-Name Island
3	120	1	20 min.	To Paradise Island—beware of tidal rips in this area
4	025	2.5	50 min.	Desolation Island—have lunch, set up camp, check weather for tomorrow's departure

Keep in mind that if you are delayed and will be overdue, it may be easier to contact the Coast Guard using your VHF radio than to contact your float plan guardian on shore. Tell the Coast Guard that you are late and they may get a call from your contact on shore. This should prevent an embarrassing and costly search-and-rescue mission.

ON-THE-WATER NAVIGATING EQUIPMENT

Despite thorough planning, Murphy's Law will still rule. Nothing ever goes quite as expected; however, planning is still a good starting point. One strategy for dealing with on-the-fly changes is to carry these basic navigation tools at all times:

Float Plan

Name_____

Address _____

City_____ State_____ Zip_____

Phone_____

Kayak type _____ Color_____ Emergency Contact No._____

Trip route: _____ to _____

Start Date_____ Time_____ End date_____

Intermediate stops:

Location_____ Expected dates_____

Location_____ Expected dates_____

Location_____ Expected dates_____

Location_____ Expected dates_____

Contingency plan _____
_____

Auto_____Color_____ Year_____ License Plate No. _____

Parking location_____

Equipment available:

Tents_____ First aid kits_____ VHF_____ Cell phones_____ GPS_____ EPIRB_____

Flares_____ Smoke_____ Dye_____ Drysuits_____Wetsuits_____ Weapons_____

Supply of food and water (in number of days) _____

Other information: _____

If expedition has not returned by:_____ at _____o'clock, please notify

_____ Phone_____

A typical float plan.

- Waterproof chart (or paper chart in a waterproof case) of the area you are paddling
- Marine deck compass
- Hiking compass
- Waterproof watch
- Waterproof paper and pencil or grease pencil for marking on the kayak hull (wrap tape around the grease pencil to keep it from deteriorating)

Additional useful items:

- GPS receiver with fresh, spare batteries
- VHF radio. Although not required for navigation, a VHF radio is an important safety tool. A cell phone can serve the same purpose if you're paddling within signal range.

ESTIMATING YOUR SPEED

The speed at which a kayaker travels varies. A kayaker's physical conditioning and skill level, the boat type and length, sea state, winds, and currents all affect speed. As a rule, longer kayaks are faster than shorter ones; the waterline length, not the total length of the kayak, determines speed. If you want to increase your speed, a different boat may help. In any event, to successfully navigate, you should know how fast you can paddle under various conditions.

One way to find out your paddling speed is to lay out a specific trip of, say, 3–5 miles and travel it under different conditions. Time yourself from start to finish and under each condition. Do it one way at a leisurely pace, then return at a faster pace. Paddle the route into the wind and return with the wind. If there are currents at that location, note them and take them into account. Do the trip in calm water as well as rough water. Record this information in a notebook to which you can refer later. You can use your results in different ways. For example, you can use your overall average speed to estimate the total time for a multi-day trip. Or to determine day-to-day speeds, you can match each day's conditions to your notebook

Below are the calculations you can use to determine speed (in knots), time (in hours), and distance (in nautical miles).

distance = speed × time traveled

speed = distance ÷ time

time = distance ÷ speed

For example, if your trip on a calm day was 5 miles, and it took you 1 hour and 15 minutes, your speed would be 4 knots (5 ÷ 1.25).

A key point to remember is that as a group, you can only travel at the speed of the slowest paddler, so he should have an accurate estimation of his speed as well. You also have to take into account socializing while on the water, sightseeing, lunch stops, etc. These will affect how long it takes to get to your destination.

Paddling speed (i.e., your speed through water) and the speed at which you actually move over the seabed floor are two different animals. The latter is referred to as *speed made good* (SMG).

Let me explain. You can expend the same amount of energy paddling against a current as you would paddling in slack water, but it will take you longer to arrive at your destination. Therefore, even though your paddling speed is the same, the rate at which you move over the seabed is different.

If you are paddling into a current or wind, your SMG will be slower; if paddling *with* the current or wind, it will be faster. An analogy to this would be a fly (named Fearless), whose flying speed is 5 mph. Let's say Fearless is a passenger on a plane traveling at 500 mph. At some point during the flight, Fearless decides to fly toward the front of the plane; as he flies, his SMG is 505 mph relative to the Earth. Then he flies toward the back of the plane; his SMG is a mere 495 mph. On the way back, he gets smacked with an in-flight magazine and drops dead to the floor. Then, even in death, Fearless's SMG is 500 mph.

Water depth also affects your speed. If you hit shallow water, say 12 to 30 inches, your speed will drop. The reason is this: as you paddle through deep water, the water passing next to your kayak moves easily downward and away, an effect called laminar flow. However, as the water depth gets shallower, the water passing below your boat hits the bottom and rebounds upward, becoming turbulent. This causes resistance or drag. The faster you try to paddle, the more drag you produce—so much so that it can take twice the effort to maintain the same speed in shallow water that you can paddle in deeper water. You will know instantly when you have reached deep water because the kayak will seem to spring forward, and you will no longer feel like you're paddling in molasses.

STAYING ON COURSE

So, now you know your paddling speed; your boat is packed; you've said good-bye to your spouse, kids, and the dog (hopefully in that order); and you're ready to start off on your glorious expedition. Following your trip table plan, you start out on leg 1 and point your kayak in the appropriate direction using the compass. The next step is to select a distant reference point and point your bow toward it. This can be a tower, hill, point of land, or even a formation of slow-moving clouds. Start paddling toward the reference point, glancing occasionally at the compass (religiously gazing at it may make you seasick) to make sure you're still on course. When one reference point outlives its usefulness, select another one in line with your original course.

Let's say you start the first leg of your trip, which is northeast at 045°M. You turn your kayak so that you're reading 045° on the compass. This is the direction you will paddle. Looking far ahead, you see a small buoy almost directly in front of you. This is your reference point. Aim for it. As you paddle, occasionally look at the compass. If it still reads 045°, and you are still heading toward the buoy, you're on course. If however, you are pointing toward the buoy but the reading has changed, or if the reading is still 045°, but you are no longer aiming at the buoy, you have drifted off course. A reference point is a target to aim for, but it won't necessarily keep you in a straight line. Sometimes drifting off course is not a big deal, sometimes it is. How can you avoid drifting off course?

Ranges

Using a range will keep you on course. *Range* is the U.S. nautical term for an alignment of objects (the UK term is *transit*). A range is useful to locate a line of position (LOP), to identify drift due to current or wind, or to help steer courses.

There are two types of ranges: *navigation* ranges and *natural* ranges. Navigation ranges are set up by the Coast Guard. Each navigation range consists of two (usually lighted) well-separated vertical markers. If a boater sees that the two markers are in alignment, he'll know he's steering a course in the center of the channel, away from hazardous areas. As a kayaker, however, it is rare that you would ever use a navigation range; channels are not safe places for small, slow boats. Instead, you'll use natural ranges. Natural ranges employ objects such as trees, rocks, mountains, or even houses, chimneys, and towers. Natural ranges aren't deliberately placed; individual boaters pick them out of their surroundings as the need arises.

Using Ranges to Determine Your Position

First let's discuss how ranges can be used to locate an LOP. Let's say that from your vantage point in the cockpit, you see a buoy that is lined up with a lighthouse in the distance. Draw a straight line across the chart intersecting both objects. That line, or LOP, will also intersect your position. If you can find an additional range, the intersection of the two LOPs will give you a fix on your location.

You can also use a single object as a range. If you can locate it on your chart, a long pier or a straight street that terminates at a boat ramp can be useful. For example, suppose you are paddling off shore and see a pier jutting out. As you pass it, there will be a point where you will be looking straight down its center. Stop and find the pier on your chart. Draw a pencil line down the center of the pier and extend it out. Now you know you are somewhere on that line.

Using Ranges to Steer Courses

Suppose you have been paddling due north. Earlier, when you had started this course, you noticed that your bow pointed toward the tip of an island and a distant tower was lined up directly behind it. Now, however, you notice that the two objects are no longer aligned; the tower lies to the right of the point of land. You've been paddling the same compass course the whole time, so what happened? This could only mean that wind or a current is moving you to the east. To compensate, you must turn the bow toward the west and paddle until the two objects line up again. You may have to paddle faster to make this happen. You'll also notice that your compass will not read the original course. As soon as you turned the bow to counteract the wind or current, your compass direction changed. Don't worry. The range will serve as a course indicator.

To better understand how to use natural ranges, let's look at the fictitious kayak trip depicted in the chart at right.

We see that the trip begins with Leg A. Janet Gudpadle and Joe Sprint put in at the river and begin to paddle Leg A. The Leg A illustration on the following page indicates what they would see from the seat of their kayaks. It's pretty much looking down the center of the river at the water tower.

The Leg B illustration shows how the area should look as they continue their paddle. Here they see that

Chart of Janet and Joe's trip.

LEG	BEARING	DISTANCE	EST. TIME
A	055°M	1.0nm	20 min.
B	015°M	1.7nm	34 min.
C	003°M	1.5nm	30 min.
D	098°M	1.6nm	32 min.
LUNCH/EXPLORE		2.0nm	2 hrs.
E	185°M	1.0nm	20 min.
F	246°M	3.3nm	1 hr.6 min.

their kayaks are aimed directly at the center of the hill on Savoy Island, with Rose Point almost in line with it.

Continuing along, Janet and Joe paddle to Rose Point and change direction to the new course for Leg C. They are now aiming toward the top left of the hill on High Island, and when they arrive adjacent to the church, they turn their kayaks to the course for Leg D, leaving the church behind.

Jan aims her kayak so the compass reads 098°, then she looks for a natural range. Well, how about that? The smaller hill on Story Island just happens to line up under the larger one (as always happens in real life—right?).

Paddling along, they keep the two hills lined up. Then about halfway across, the smaller hill starts to look larger than the one behind it as their perspective changes.

In the final sketch, the original range has disappeared, but as luck would have it,

Leg A: *The perspective from the kayak seat.*

Leg B: *Janet and Joe aim directly at Savoy Island.*

Leg C: *Heading toward High Island.*

Leg D: *Starting Out. The natural range from this perspective is the alignment of the two hills on Story Island.*

Leg D: *Midway. Perspective makes the smaller hill in front appear larger than the hill behind it.*

Leg D: *Almost There. As they get closer, the kayakers must pick a new natural range.*

there is a tall tree on the shore directly under the top of the smaller hill. These two points become the new range. And if they have not been pushed off course by wind or waves, the compass should still read 098°.

Reaching the lunch spot for a well-deserved break, Jan pats herself on the back for her navigational skills. After lunch, they continue to paddle and explore around the islands. Leaving the far point of land on the east side of Duck Island, they paddle for about 20 minutes on a heading of 185 degrees. Jan thinks they should be approximately where the circle is on the chart, but then she notices the current symbol she jotted down when she was preplanning the trip. It indicates 1 knot at 306 degrees (refer back to Chart of Janet and Joe's trip).

> "How do we figure our actual position?" Joe asks.
> "We can't. However we can get a reasonable estimate using dead reckoning." Janet replies. "If we had been paddling for an hour at 185°M we would have gone about 3 miles." Janet marks the dead reckoning (DR) position of where they should have been on the chart with a half circle. She continues, "Due to the current, we also would have been pushed 1 nautical mile at an angle of about 306 . . ."

"Degrees," Joe says. "But we've only paddled for 20 minutes or a third of an hour, so we've only gone 1 mile and have only drifted a third of a mile."

"Right," Jan responds as she marks their new estimated position (EP) on the chart with a pencilled-in triangle or square around the position dot. They plot a new course on the chart toward the mouth of the river and head for home.

5 Navigating in Fog and Wind

FOG

FOG IS BASICALLY ONE OF TWO TYPES: *RADIATION FOG* or *sea fog*. Radiation fog (also called *ground fog*), usually burns off after an hour or two, has no wind connected with it, and generally doesn't provide kayakers with much to worry about. Sea fog, on the other hand, usually comes with strong winds, can cover hundreds of miles, and may last for days on end. Sea fog does not burn off.

> *Everybody ought to do at least two things each day that he or she hates to do, just for practice.*
>
> WILLIAM JAMES

Your senses of hearing and, to some extent, smell are all you have to guide you through fog. And it's often difficult to determine the direction of sounds in a fog. Be aware that boats, including kayaks, are required by law to sound horns (see table on the following page) in any reduced visibility, both during the day and at night, but many times smaller boats do not adhere to this law, so you may not see them until it is too late. The following table is taken from the U.S. Coast Guard Rules of Navigation. (For more definitive information, refer to Rules of Navigation online; see Appendix B, Online Navigation Resources.)

Generally you can see fog banks move in. They often come in on the tide, with a breeze from seaward. If fog is closing in, locate your present position as accurately as possible while you can still see landmarks. If you are out of sight of landmarks, explore the possibility of getting closer to shore, providing there are no rocks, dumping surf, or boat traffic with which to contend. In any event, establish your location as best you can.

Piloting without visibility is not possible in a kayak (except when using a GPS), and your only choice is dead reckoning. Even starting with a good navigational fix, over a period of time, your position will become more uncertain. If you haven't

Horn Signals			
VESSEL LENGTH	MOVING OR STOPPED	SIGNAL	INTERVAL
Over 39.4 feet (12 meters)	Moving	1 long (4 to 6 seconds in duration)	Less than 2 minutes
Over 39.4 feet (12 meters)	Moving but restricted in maneuverability	1 long, 2 short	Less than 2 minutes
Over 39.4 feet (12 meters)	Stopped	2 long—2 seconds apart	Less than 2 minutes
Under 39.4 feet (12 meters)	May use any of the above signals or must make other sound signal		Less than 2 minutes

been paying attention and can't get a good fix, you will soon become quite lost. If you are in a group, have each member check their compass reading with one another to determine accuracy. Assign each person a number, so if you lose visual contact with one another, you can call for a head count at regular intervals, with each person saying their number aloud.

Head for a safe destination on shore, but do not aim directly for this haven unless there is absolutely no wind or current. Aim for the upwind or up-current end so that you have a better chance of not missing it. In addition, if you aim off your target, you will have a better idea of knowing which way to turn to find it when you do reach shore.

Estimate your paddling speed, factor in any wind or currents, and get an idea of how long it will take you to reach your destination. You should try to include aiming for buoys along the way. These will act as checks on your progress. Sound buoys may aid you if you can hear them. But because they are activated by wind or wave action, they may not make any sound in the calm water that is sometimes associated with fog.

This is a situation where knowledge of your paddling speed becomes important. Let's assume your normal paddling speed is 3.5 knots, but it can vary from as low as 3.0 to as high as 4.0 knots under certain conditions. This means that in two hours of paddling, your distance traveled could be anywhere from 6 to 8 miles. You must consider this range difference in your estimated time calculations.

The same holds true for wind or currents moving you off course. Let's say you decide to head for an island to wait out the fog, and you allow for a 1-knot cross current. If, in fact, the cross current is 1.5 knots, and you paddle for two hours, you may miss the island by a mile (0.5 kt x 2 hr). Try not to cross any strong currents in the fog if possible. The goal is to get to an area where you know you can safely hole up or paddle along the shore until the fog lifts.

If you are caught in fog and *know for sure that you are very close* to your target, but you can't quite see it, you may be able to find it using the following procedure:

1. Start paddling at 0, 120, or 240 degrees (these are easier to mentally calculate); use whichever one you believe is closest to your target. Paddle for about 1 minute.
2. Add 120 degrees and paddle for 2 minutes.
3. Add another 120 degrees and paddle for 3 minutes.
4. Continue this procedure until you arrive at your destination.

Each minute you paddle (assuming 3 knots speed), you travel a little over 300 feet (1 nm = 6000 ft; 3 nm = 18,000 ft; 18,000 ft ÷ 60 minutes = 300 ft), and your triangle grows each cycle. This is a good method for finding smaller islands, such as the 300-foot island in the illustration. If the island is larger, you can increase the time spread accordingly. For example, paddle 2 minutes on Leg 1, 4 minutes on Leg 2, and so on. The distance between the passes will be greater but because the island is larger, it is unlikely that you will miss it.

If you were approximately 1,000 feet from the island or about ⅙th of a nautical mile, it would take

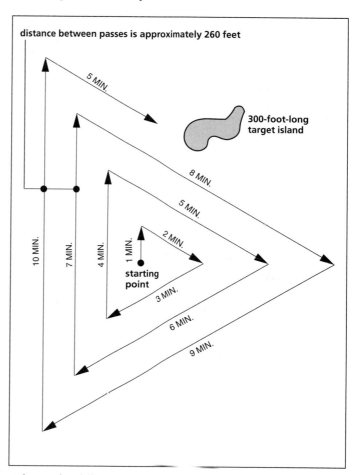

When in fog, follow this pattern to find an object close to you.

you about one hour to locate the island using this procedure. However, you may possibly hear the surf, leaves rustling in trees, or other signs of your target on Leg 5. If so, start the sequence all over again from your present position, and you might find the island a little quicker.

WIND—LOVE IT OR HATE IT

Wind is an important factor to take into account when planning a trip. Unlike a current, wind is unpredictable. It can change from minute to minute, making it hard to plan for. Wind can blow you off course and, if strong enough, severely affect your speed, if not stop it completely. It will grab at large-bladed paddles, creating the potential for capsizing. As wind speed increases, the forces applied against your boat, body, and paddle increase tremendously! We've all heard weather forecasts like "Winds SW 15–20 mph, with gusts to 25;" have you ever experienced these winds on the water?

Understanding wind can help you compensate for its effects. Some winds can even be beneficial. A moderate tailwind can increase your speed and reduce your effort. Some kayakers have used kites to pull their kayak through the water with the wind. And some kayaks can be equipped with sails.

Wind Direction

Denoting wind direction can be confusing. A west wind, for example, is defined differently than a west current. Wind direction is identified by the direction from which the wind is coming, while current is identified by the direction to which the water is flowing. Therefore, a west wind is exactly the opposite direction than a west current. If you find yourself in conditions of opposing wind and current (referred to as *wind against tide*), you will encounter steep waves that break sooner and form whitecaps.

Wind Speed and Apparent Wind

It is also important to understand the difference between wind speed and apparent wind. To picture this, let's go back to our friend, Fearless the Fly. On his way to the airport, Fearless stopped to have a bite to eat from some nice lady's breakfast dish. As he was sitting there, he noticed the wind picked up. Fearless estimated the wind was hitting his body at 20 mph (he's good at estimating).

Fearless realized he couldn't fly against such strong winds, so he jumped onto the roof of a taxi heading toward the airport and held on tightly. The taxi drove at 30 mph into the 20-mph wind and, even though the actual wind speed had not changed, Fearless now felt the wind hitting his body at 50 mph. This is called *apparent wind*.

Fearless was tiring quickly. Just when thought he could no longer keep a grip, the taxi slowed, made a couple of turns, and now traveled at a speed of 20 mph in the same direction as the wind. Fearless barely had to hold on anymore. The taxi was traveling at the same speed and direction as the wind, so he now felt the apparent wind as 0 mph.

You may have noticed this effect yourself if you ever rode a bike on a windy day in the summer sun. As you are going with the wind, you really seem to be moving, but you have sweat on your face and feel hot because there is little or no apparent wind. You turn around and paddle the same speed into the wind. It now requires more work to maintain the speed, but you feel cooler.

Compensating for Wind

Wind demands strong consideration when navigating. If you don't compensate for the wind, you'll be blown off course.

For starters, wind is more irksome than current. Both will be moving you off course, but the wind can change the orientation of the boat by constantly pushing the bow toward the wind. This effect is called *weather cocking* and is common in most kayak designs. When a kayak is moving forward, the bow is somewhat anchored by the bow wave (as shown in the illustration). The stern is in a type of low-pressure area, where the water is flowing back in to fill the hole that the boat just made by displacing the water. This gives the stern more freedom to move than the bow.

The result is that when the wind is hitting the kayak on the beam or quartering into it, it can push the stern away easier than it can the bow. So the bow doesn't actually turn into the wind, but rather the stern swings away from it. The result: the kayak turns towards the wind.

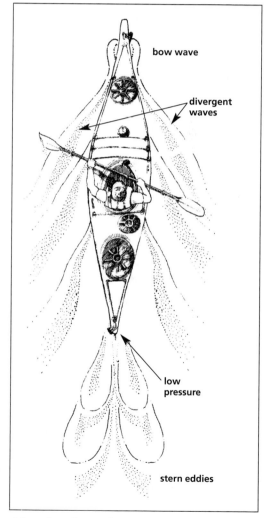

A kayak in forward motion.

This situation will cause you to expend a good deal of energy in trying to keep the boat on course. You can reduce the effect to a certain degree. It may not be much, but, hey, we need all the help we can get out there. If your kayak has a rudder or skeg, use it. It adds lateral resistance, and the wind cannot push the stern around as much.

Some tips to follow, whether or not your kayak has a rudder or skeg:

- Extend your paddle on the downwind side. This makes a longer lever for counteracting the effects of the wind.
- Use power strokes on the windward side of the kayak and sweep strokes on the downwind side.
- Tilt or edge your kayak, using your legs and body, so the high side is away from the wind direction. For example, if the wind is from the starboard side, lift your left leg and compress your body on the left side so you are sitting on your right buttock.

You can also minimize the effect of the wind by loading the kayak for the prevailing conditions. If you want to go upwind, load the kayak slightly bow heavy. The stern will be raised higher and will act similar to a weathervane, keeping the bow pointed upwind. If you want to go downwind, load the kayak stern heavy. This will raise the bow higher, causing it to act as the weathervane, pointing you downwind.

How the Wind Affects You

Wind affects your kayak and speed in a number of ways. Headwinds decrease your SMG; tailwinds increase it. Quartering winds affect both speed and course to varying degrees, depending on the angle.

How much of an increase or decrease in speed depends on several variables, but if you normally travel at a rate of 3 knots, a 25-knot headwind can decrease your speed by 50% or more. You may only be able to make 1 to 1½ knots. At 40 knots of wind, you might make no headway at all.

Traveling downwind, a 25-knot wind can increase your effective speed to 4 knots or more. The effect of a tailwind does not offer as much propelling power as do the waves they usually form. A following sea causes the stern to be raised higher than the bow, so the boat slides down the face of the wave by gravity. When it hits the trough, the bow digs in, and the kayak stops until another wave lifts the stern up again.

The procedure for making headway in this type of sea is to paddle down the face and to not waste energy paddling in the trough. Be cautious not to broach (turn sideways), or you may capsize. This happens more often in larger waves. Although following seas feel quite disorienting to less experienced kayakers, they are a blessing to an old pro. The reason for this is that an experienced kayaker will realize a dramatic increase in SMG with little effort—and it's fun.

When a crosswind affects your course, it doesn't have the same effect as a current. If you were in a 10-knot current, you would be propelled downstream at the same rate as the water. In slack water with a 10-knot wind, it's probable that you may only be moved one knot or less, assuming you did not alter your course to compensate.

Estimating Wind Speed

Although Fearless the Fly was good at estimating, most people cannot even come close to guessing the wind speed. Fortunately we can get a marine forecast from the television or radio, purchase an anemometer (wind meter), or use the Beaufort scale on the following page, which relates observable land and sea states to wind speed. With the Beaufort Scale, you don't even need batteries. It's a good idea to make a copy of the Beaufort Scale, then laminate it and keep it on deck. Try guessing the wind speed from the objects around you, then look at the scale to see how accurate you are. Look at the flag in the photo below. Notice it appears to be a medium size flag and is somewhat extended? Judging by the Beaufort Scale, the wind must be between Force 3 and a Force 4.

The appearance of this flag indicates a Force 3 or 4 wind.

Of course you must also take into consideration the other things around you. Are the tops of trees swaying? What do the waves look like? By mentally taking note of all these things, you can get a fairly good idea of the force of the wind. After all, this is what mariners have been doing for a long, long time.

Beaufort Scale

BEAUFORT NUMBER: FORCE	WIND SPEED IN KNOTS (MPH)*	SEAMAN'S TERM	SEA STATE	EFFECTS ON LAND	EFFECTS ON PADDLING**
0	Less than 1	Calm	Sea like glass, flat, calm.	Calm; smoke rises vertically.	Easy going, perhaps boring for some. Good canoeing on sheltered bay. Practice your edging.
1	1 to 3 (1 to 3.5)	Light air	Ripples with appearance of scales; no foam crests.	Smoke drifts with wind direction; weathervanes do not move.	Still easy to kayak or canoe. Go fishing from your boat. Perfect your strokes.
2	4 to 6 (4.5 to 7)	Light breeze	Small wavelets (6"–8"). Crests have glassy appearance; no breaking waves.	Wind is felt on face; weathervanes do not move; leaves rustle.	Novices learn what weathercocking is all about. Experienced paddlers can still canoe.
3	7 to 10 (8 to 11.5)	Gentle breeze	Large wavelets (2'). Crests begin to break; scattered whitecaps.	Leaves, small twigs move; small flags extended.	Good for intermediate paddlers to practice in. Fun trip for most. Take the canoe home. Buy a kayak.
4	11 to 16 (12.5 to 18.5)	Moderate breeze	Small waves (3') with numerous whitecaps.	Dust, paper, leaves raised up. Small branches move. Medium flags extended.	Novices worry. Early intermediates may be apprehensive. Experienced paddlers have lots of fun.
5	17 to 21 (19.5 to 24)	Fresh breeze	Moderate waves (6') with many whitecaps and some spray.	Small trees in leaf sway. Large flags ripple.	Novices watch TV. Hard paddling into wind for most kayakers. Intermediates worry especially in following seas. Rescues are not easy.

Beaufort Scale (cont.)

BEAUFORT NUMBER: FORCE	*WIND SPEED IN KNOTS (MPH)	SEAMAN'S TERM	SEA STATE	EFFECTS ON LAND	**EFFECTS ON PADDLING
6	22 to 27 (25 to 31)	Strong breeze	Larger waves (10'); whitecaps everywhere with much spray.	Larger branches of trees in motion; whistling can be heard in wires and sailboat rigging.	Small craft warnings. Intermediates watch TV. Experienced kayakers wish they were watching TV. Rescues become difficult.
7	28 to 33 (32 to 38)	Moderate gale	Large waves (13'); foam blown in streaks. Sea heaps up.	Whole trees are in motion, resistance felt while walking against wind.	Headway very difficult. Hard to turn. Wind may rip paddle from kayaker. It is very difficult to communicate.
8	34 to 40 (39 to 46)	Fresh gale	Moderately high waves (18') with longer length. Crests break into spindrift.	Small branches and twigs are broken off. Hard walking against wind.	It's every man and woman for themselves. Constant battle to paddle. Kayak rescues are a miracle if they happen at all.
9	41 to 47 (47 to 54)	Strong gale	High waves (23'). Sea begins to roll; visibility affected.	Light structural damage occurs. Roof shingles torn from roofs.	Intermediates dream they can handle this. Advanced have nightmares thinking about it. Kayak rescues are all but impossible.
10	48 to 55 (55 to 63)	Whole gale or storm	Very high waves (30'); sea looks white as foam is blown in dense streaks; heavy sea roll. Visibility is restricted.	Moderate structural damage occurs. Some trees uprooted.	This is a survival situation. The only options, which may or may not work, are running before the wind or using a sea anchor.
11	56 to 63 (72.5 to 72.5)	Violent storm	Exceptionally high waves (35'). Visibility is poor.	Heavy widespread structural damage. Large trees uprooted.	Agnostics start praying.

(continued next page)

Beaufort Scale (cont.)

BEAUFORT NUMBER: FORCE	WIND SPEED IN KNOTS (MPH)*	SEAMAN'S TERM	SEA STATE	EFFECTS ON LAND	EFFECTS ON PADDLING**
12	Over 64 (74)	Hurricane	Waves may reach 45' in height. Foam and spray in the air makes for very poor visibility.	Very heavy structural damage. Coastal areas evacuated. Very large trees broken or uprooted.	Atheists who swear there is no heaven suddenly find religion.

* 1 knot equals approximately 1.15 statute miles per hour

** Effects on paddling depend on many factors; whether wind is onshore or offshore, sheltered waters or open sea, skill level of kayaker, fetch, duration, etc.

6 Putting it Together

NOW THAT WE KNOW SOME OF THE BASICS, HOW DO we put all this information together? Obviously it does us no good if we are not prepared. The first thing to do is plan the trip and make a trip table as discussed in Chapter 4. Decide where you will launch from, the compass direction, and the distance and estimated time of each leg of the route. You can write this information on a piece of paper and protect it in a clear, sealed plastic bag. Or you can write it directly on the kayak deck using a grease pencil, which works quite well. On a dark colored boat, use a white china marker.

While underway, take note of the wind intensity, wind direction, and current behavior. Make allowances for these in your headings and time allotted. Try to determine how long it will take you to reach each of these places. Follow the course by casting an occasional eye on the compass. If possible, refer to a natural or man-made range to maintain this course. By repeating this procedure for every leg of the journey, you should reach your destination within a short time of your estimate.

The best trips are well planned by making allowances for the conditions that will affect you. If you had to cross a bay that was 9 miles wide from point A to point B, you could arrange the trip in any number of ways.

SCENARIO 1

After plotting your course, check the time of high, low, and slack water for the area. Try to find the speed of the current from either current tables or local knowledge. Listen to the marine forecast and determine if the weather is conducive to the trip.

If the flood and ebb currents are roughly the same, an easy way to make the crossing is to plan to be halfway across at slack water.

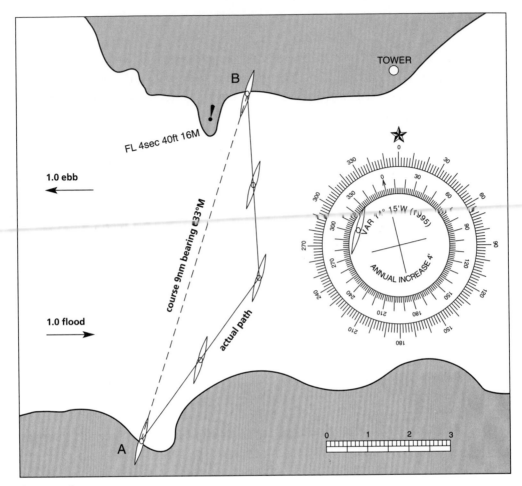

Labels in image: TOWER; B; FL 4sec 40ft 16M; 1.0 ebb; 1.0 flood; course 9nm bearing 33°M; actual path; A; VAR 14° 15'W (1995); ANNUAL INCREASE 4'; 0 1 2 3

Scenario 1.

Assume slack water is at about 12 noon, and a 9-mile crossing at approximately 3 mph takes 3 hours. If you leave 1½ hours before slack water, at about 10:30 A.M., the flood current will take you to the right for half the trip, and the ebb will bring you back the second half. This may be disorienting as you paddle because your kayak will appear to be drifting toward the tower as the current carries you to the right for the first half of the crossing. Midway the current will reverse, and you will be crabbing back toward your intended landfall, *even though the kayak is not pointed toward it.* You must follow the plotted course using your compass rather than aiming for a target. In this scenario, you will not have to alter your compass reading of 33°. (Determine this number by aligning the course line over the center of the compass rose and reading the course off the magnetic scale.)

SCENARIO 2

Let's suppose you cannot wait for slack water and must cross during the ebb. A local fisherman has told you the ebb current averages 1 knot. If you paddle on the course line of 033°M and the trip takes 3 hours to get across, then in that amount of time, the current will move you about 3 miles downstream of your target as shown in this first illustration below. What can you do to correct this problem?

One answer is to select a point 3 miles upstream of your intended destination, take a compass bearing to that point and turn the bow of your kayak to that heading. The following illustration shows your kayak aiming for a point 3 miles upstream at a heading of 048°M. Stick to this compass reading. You are pointed

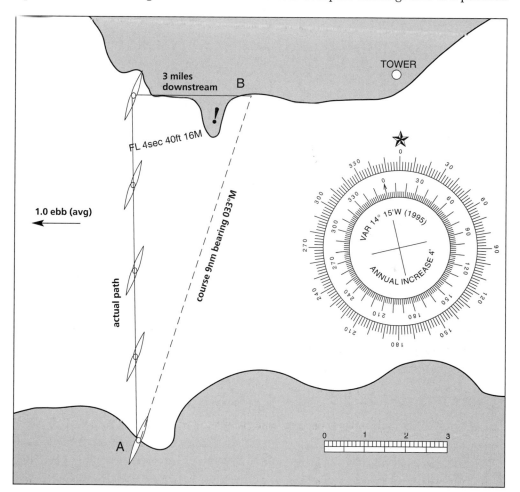

Secnario 2. In this illustration, the current speed of 1 knot and travel of time of 3 hours mean you will be moved about 3 miles downstream.

almost directly at the tower (as seen in the second illustration below) and the ebb current should cause you to end up just about where you intended.

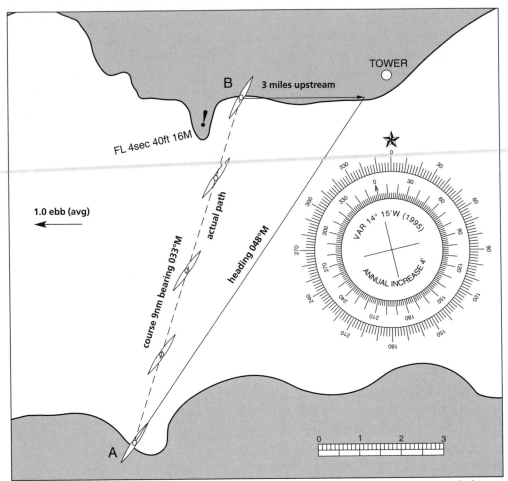

Scenario 2 (continued). To compensate, aim for a point 3 miles upstream of your intended destination.

SCENARIO 3

For this scenario, assume the current speeds are not constant, so you must include the 50/90 rule in your calculations. If you start your crossing the 4th hour after slack, the flow will be at 90% of maximum. Midway across at the 5th hour, the flow will be at 50%, and for the final hour of your crossing, the flow will be at 0% or slack water.

You can calculate the crossing in stages to determine more accurately the headings you need to paddle (as shown in the figure below), but it takes more time and steps to calculate and monitor than it's worth.

It is much easier to add the flows together and work with that. Add the current flow rates for the period of time you expect to be doing the crossing, and the sum will tell you how far the current will move you.

The table on the following page shows the current information (50/90 rule) for the crossing. At the 3rd hour after slack, the current runs at 100%, but our 1st hour of the crossing starts at the 4th hour after slack which is at 90% or 1.35 knots. Our 2nd hour is the 5th hour after slack at 50% or 0.75 knots. Our final hour is at 0% or slack water.

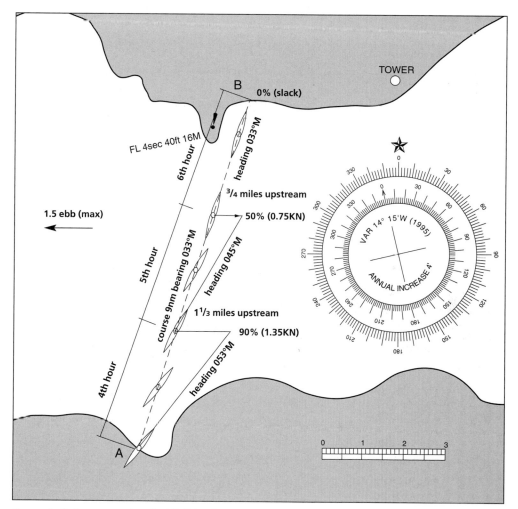

Scenario 3. Incorporating the 50/90 rule.

50/90 Rule as Applied to Scenario 3		
HOURS AFTER SLACK	**PERCENT**	**KNOTS**
Slack	0	0
1	50	0.75
2	90	1.35
3	100	1.50
4 (1st hour of trip)	90	1.35
5 (2nd hour of trip)	50	0.75
6 (3rd hour of trip)	0	0

Adding 1.35 + 0.75 + 0.00 equals 2.10 nautical miles. This is how far you would drift with the ebb current over the 3-hour period. All you have to do for this crossing is to measure 2.1 nautical miles upstream of your target, take a bearing to that point, and turn your boat to that heading. Keep to that compass reading as you paddle. Your boat will be pointing east of your intended destination, but the current will set you to the west, so your actual path will be a nearly straight line to your destination at Point B.

What if the crossing took longer, and you were out for 4 hours during the 4th, 5th, and 6th hour of the ebb tide and the 1st hour of the flood? You would add the total flows of the ebb and subtract the flood as shown in the table on the following page.

The result is that you would be moved 1.35 knots in the ebb direction. Set your compass course to a point that is 1.35 miles upstream.

SCENARIO 4

You can also attack this exercise in another manner. In many places close to shore, the water will actually be running back upstream opposite to the main current. This is known as a back eddy, and you can use this to your advantage. Even if there is no back eddy, in most cases, the current will be moving at a slower rate the closer you are to shore.

In the illustration on page 84, we first move the course line 3 miles upstream without changing the course bearing. The reason for this is that a 9-mile crossing at approximately 3 mph takes 3 hours, and at a 1-knot current, it would move you downstream 3 miles.

50/90 rule—Exercise 2 (Scenario 2)

HOURS AFTER SLACK	PERCENT	KNOTS
Slack	0	0
1	50	0.75
2	90	1.35
3	100	1.50
4 (1st hour of trip)	90	1.35
5 (2nd hour of trip)	50	0.75
6 (3rd hour of trip)	0	0
1 (4th hour of trip)	50 (Flood)	0.75
Total ebb flow (4th, 5th, 6th hours)		2.10
Minus Total flood flow (1st hour)		0.75
Difference (Ebb wins)		1.35

We then use the back eddy to make our way upstream closely following the coastline (provided it is safe to do so) to the point where the course line intersects the coast. From this alternate launch point, we head the kayak on the original course of 033° and allow the current to take us downstream to our target.

In this particular example though, when you get to the alternate launch point, the distance across is now shorter. It will take you less time to cross, so be sure to allow for that.

THE FLY IN THE OINTMENT

Admittedly, I am using simplistic approaches in these exercises, and there are many ways to do this crossing. Everyone has their own favorite methods and as long as it works for them, that's fine. There are many good navigational books that will teach you other methods. I sincerely encourage you to read up on them. However, personally, when learning something new, I like to keep it simple.

The previous examples work fine when currents are not particularly fast, but they do not take into account one important factor. As you angle into the current, it

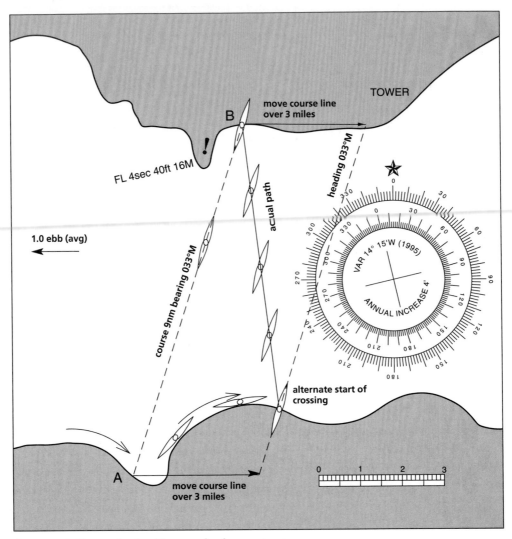

TOWER

move course line
over 3 miles

B

heading 033°M

FL 4sec 40ft 16M

aCual path

1.0 ebb (avg)

course 9nm bearing 033°M

VAR 14° 15'W (1995)

ANNUAL INCREASE 4'

alternate start of
crossing

A

move course line
over 3 miles

0   1   2   3

Scenario 4. Using a back eddy to make the crossing.

reduces your speed somewhat; therefore, instead of a 3-hour crossing, it takes 3 hours and 10 minutes. This extra bit gives the current more time to push you off course, and you should compensate for this factor by angling upstream a little more.

There is a way to approximate what your actual speed across will be, along with the new heading to take. It involves vectors and a little math. Don't let it scare you, it's really pretty simple. It is called a ferry angle calculation. There are four steps, and all you need to perform it is a pencil and a small piece of paper, so gather them up and get ready for the next chapter.

7 Ferry Angle Calculation

O N-WATER NAVIGATION FROM YOUR KAYAK IS QUITE different from the planning you do back home. In the real world, currents and wind make it difficult to follow your plan. The ferry angle calculation will give you a good estimation of how to counteract the currents.

A ferry glide, or ferrying, is a procedure where the kayaker paddles into the current to offset its effects. If there is little current, the angle will be shallow, but as the current increases, the angle into it must also increase. River kayakers use this method all the time for crossing rivers or, more often, to get to those great play spots.

In the previous chapter, we discussed some strategies for handling currents. As was mentioned earlier, if the current is opposing you, then your SMG is decreased, and if it's flowing with you, your SMG is increased. If it's directly opposing you at the same speed you are paddling, then your SMG is zero. If it exceeds your paddling speed, then you are going backwards, and you'll never arrive at your destination.

For sea kayakers making a long crossing where no natural ranges are visible, ferrying into a moderate to fast current is not easy. Even with knowledge of the current speeds and direction, you must remember they will not be exact. Tidal velocities vary, depending upon whether it is a spring or a neap tide or if it is in-between those times. And they vary with your distance from shore—currents move faster in deeper water. If you have no visual reference, it is extremely difficult to tell how the current (or wind) is affecting you.

Even so, knowing how to calculate the ferry angle is quite useful. Even with these variables, you can often get quite close to your target, if not dead on. Most times, it will get you close enough to allow you to spot your target and adjust your

> *I know God will not give me anything I can't handle. I just wish that He didn't trust me so much.*
>
> MOTHER TERESA

direction as needed. By that time, you should be able to pick up a range and use that to control your line of travel.

To start with, we need to know the speed and direction that the current will be flowing during your crossing. In Chapter 3, Tides and Tidal Currents, there was a sample of the current tables that showed this information. Sometimes charts will show the flow diagrams right on them. The angle at which the arrow is drawn on the chart indicates the direction of flow.

ESTIMATING YOUR SMG

The following exercises show how to estimate your SMG. In these exercises, you are heading once again from Point A to Point B, but this time the direction of the current is different, and the distance is 4 nautical miles across. You notice that the 1-knot current is coming at you from behind at an an angle now, effectively increasing your speed. You must calculate the SMG along with the new heading to offset this current. This is called a ferry angle calculation.

First get a small piece of paper, no particular size, and a pencil. Fold the paper in at least four equal parts as shown in the photo.

You can draw lines on the folds if you wish.

Each of these divisions or units can represent any rate of speed you wish. They can be 0.25 knots or 0.5 knots; whatever is convenient for you. If you made them 0.5 knots, the paper will only be long enough to accommodate a speed of 2 knots (4 folds at ½ knot = 2 knots), so you may have to fold it again for it to be useful. Having the units as 1-knot increments works out well for our purposes. Keep in mind that you cannot use this folded paper to measure distance on your chart. It is a speed scale.

Fold the paper so as to end up with four parts.

Step 1. Draw the course line on the chart. In this exercise, it is 033°M.

Step 2. Place a corner of your piece of paper on the course line (preferably near the destination or the end of the paddling leg) and draw the current line to match the angle of flow shown on the chart or as obtained from the current tables. The angle of our current line is 68 degrees. You should also draw the length of the current line to match the speed of the current (see illustration below). Draw the line 1 unit long to represent the current speed of 1 knot. If we knew the current speed was 1.5 knots, we would draw it 1½ units long.

Step 3. Add the paddling speed line (see illustration on page 88). Let's assume your paddling speed is 3 knots. Place one end of your paper scale at the end of the current line you just drew, and rotate the paper until the three-units line (representing your paddling speed) crosses the course line. Draw a line along the edge of the paper

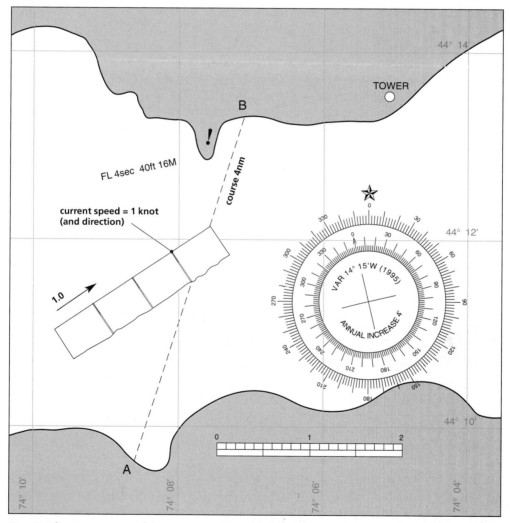

Step 2: Place one corner of the paper on the course line and draw on the current line. The length of the line matches the speed of the current.

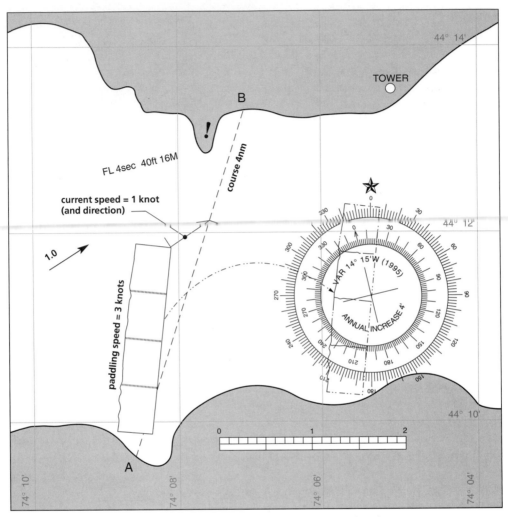

Step 3: Add the paddling speed line, which also becomes your new heading.

scale. This paddling speed line is also the angle that you should paddle. If you slide it over the compass rose, you will see that you should paddle on a bearing of 020°M.

Step 4. By adding the current line and the paddling speed line to the course line, you have created a triangle. To determine your estimated SMG, use the paper scale to measure the leg of the triangle formed by the course line (see illustration on page 89). In this case, it's about 3.75 knots. To calculate crossing time:

distance ÷ SMG = crossing time (in hours)
4 nm ÷ 3.75 kt = 1.067 hr

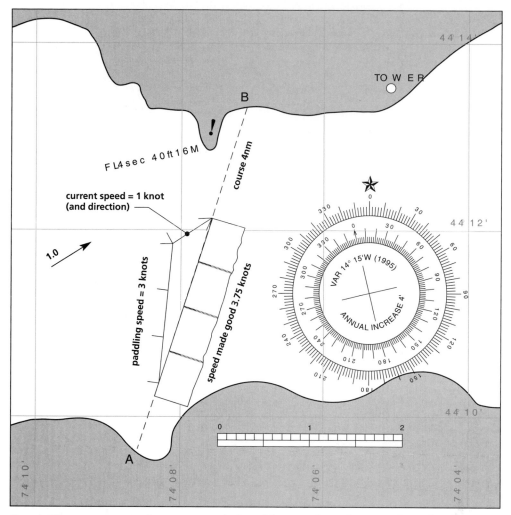

Step 4: Use your paper scale to measure the leg of the triangle on the course line. This determines your SMG.

Therefore, it should take a little more than one hour to make the crossing.

This exercise had the current more or less going with us, thereby increasing our speed. The illustration on page 90 depicts the ferry angle calculation with the current against us. As you study the diagram, you will notice that the current will decrease your SMG to approximately 2.25 knots, and the trip will take 1.8 hours.

Finally in the illustration on page 91, the current speed is 4 knots, and your paddling speed is 3 knots. Notice that the paddling speed line cannot reach the course line, in this exercise, you will never reach point B directly.

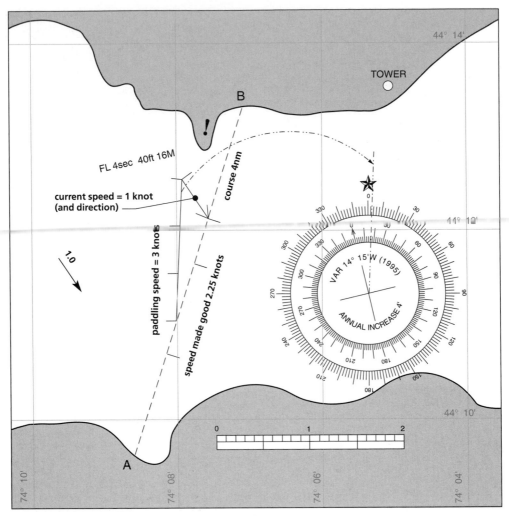

Determining the ferry angle calculation when the current is against you.

APPROXIMATING YOUR HEADING

You've just seen how to use a piece of paper and a pencil to determine your SMG as well as a new heading when paddling in currents. If you only need to approximate your heading, there is a simple calculation that will let you do it quickly. However, you still need to have a good idea of the speed of the current.

Current Perpendicular to Direction of Travel

Use the formula below if the current is close to being perpendicular (on the beam) to your course. For example, the current is coming from the right at 1.5 knots and is

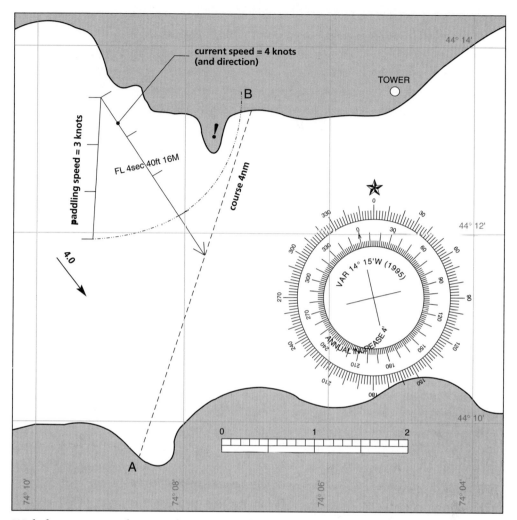

With the current speed greater than your paddling speed, you will not reach Point B directly.

perpendicular to your course. You are paddling at 4 knots, and your course is 030°M (see illustration). Do the math:

(current speed ÷ paddling speed) × 60 = angle required
(1.5 kt ÷ 4 kt) × 60 = 22.5°

Use 22 degrees because you can't paddle to half-degree increments. Turn the kayak 22 degrees toward the up-current side. (Since the current is coming from our right, turning the compass to the up-current side will add to our course. If the

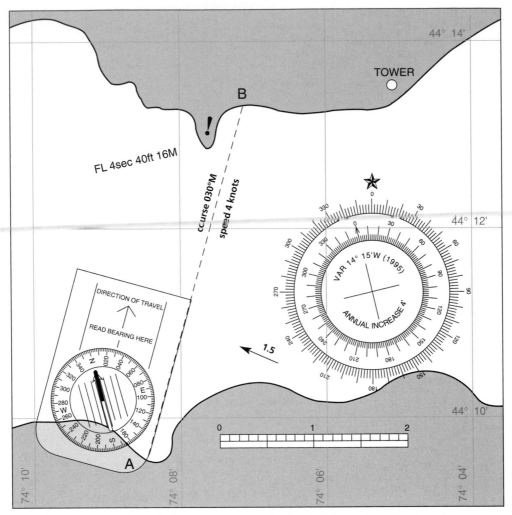

Calculating your heading when current is perpendicular (90 degrees) to direction of travel.

current were coming from our left, turning the compass would subtract from our course, and our heading would be 008°M.) In our exercise, the compass now reads 052 degrees (see next page).

Current 45 Degrees to Direction of Travel

If the current is closer to being 45 degrees forward of the beam (on the bow) or 45 degrees aft of the beam (on the quarter) to your course, then use 40 (rather than 60) as the multiplier in the formula.

For this exercise, assume your paddling speed is 3 knots, and a 1-knot current is hitting your kayak on the quarter (or on the bow) at approximately 45 degrees.

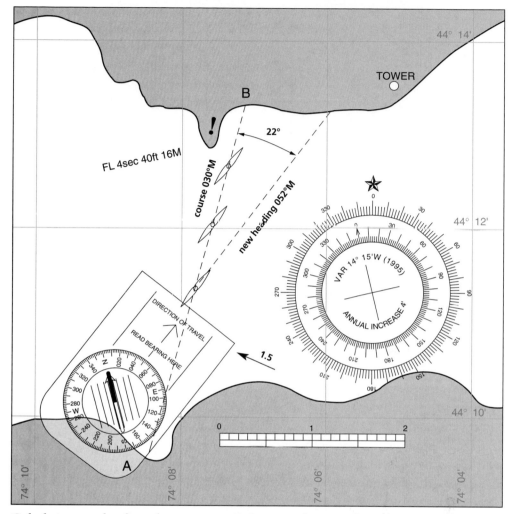

Calculating your heading when current is 45 degrees to direction of travel.

(current speed ÷ paddling speed) × 40 = angle required
(1.0 kt ÷ 3 kt) × 40 = 13.3°

If the original course bearing is at 033 degrees, then subtract 13 degrees (turning left toward the up-current side) for a result of 020 degrees (which was the result in our vector solution; see illustration for step 3 of the ferry angle calculation, page 88).

Of course, if you have visual landmarks you can use as a natural range, you can adjust your angle so that the objects always remain aligned, as discussed back in Chapter 4, Preparing to Paddle.

8 Pre-Navigation

I was never as good as all the credit I got, and never as bad as the criticism I received.

ROGER SMITH

I CAN HEAR IT NOW, "PRE-NAVIGATION? WHAT IN THE world does he mean by that." Well, whatever you want to call it, the process of pre-navigation is a great way to keep things simple. Often overlooked in books or articles about navigation, it is one of the best pre-trip planning exercises you can do. You've heard it said of someone who's on the ball that "He's done his homework." This is exactly what pre-navigation is: doing one's homework before the big test. You may want to do this in addition to plotting out your courses and making your trip table as discussed earlier.

As was mentioned in previous chapters, there is not a whole lot of room on the deck of a kayak for working out navigation problems. What was easy to do at home with a series of large charts, on a flat surface, with the proper plotting instruments, becomes quite difficult using small charts or portions of charts on a surface that is tiny, usually curved, and wet at that. In rough seas, it can become virtually impossible. You need every advantage you can get. Pre-navigation qualifies as an advantage. By doing this prep work at home, you won't have to put into practice the exercise discussed in Chapter 2, "Finding Where You Are on the Chart."

Briefly put, we want to draw radiating lines from each of the targets at convenient intervals and write the magnetic bearings to them (to agree with the direction from which we would view the object in our kayaks). These lines should cover the area we intend to paddle. We will use 10-degree increments for this exercise. If this became too crowded, we could use 20-degree increments.

For this method to be effective, a few conditions must be met:

- There must be a minimum of two targets, but preferably three, appearing on your chart that you can see from the water. The closer they are at right angles to one another, as viewed from your location, the more accurate your position fix will be.
- Your boat must be equipped with a deck compass, or you must have a hand compass and know how to take a bearing.
- You must have good visibility.
- You must have a basic knowledge of navigation. If you've made it this far, you qualify.

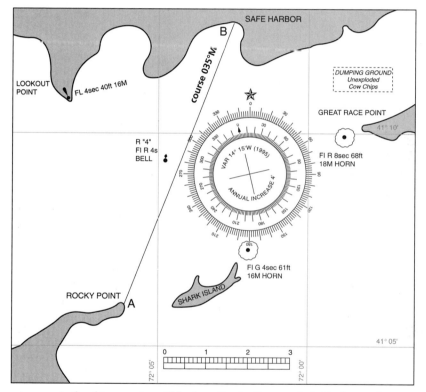

Our imaginary trip for this exercise will be from Rocky Point to Safe Harbor, a distance of approximately 8 miles. Looking at our chart (above), we see that there are three lights that should be visible to us as we paddle: Great Race Point Lighthouse, Shark Island Lighthouse, and the light at Lookout Point.

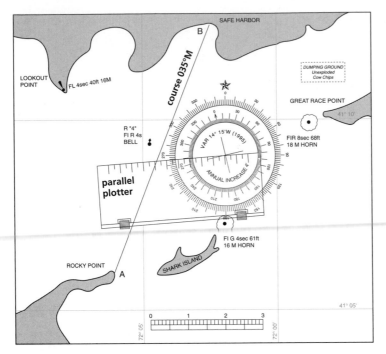

Align your parallel tool over the center of the compass rose and start at, say, the 100-degree mark on the magnetic compass scale as shown.

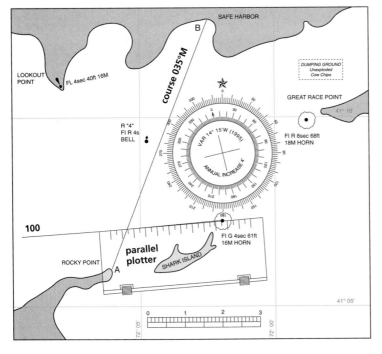

Next we roll the parallel tool over the center of the Shark Island Lighthouse and draw a line from it. Write the bearing (100°M) to the lighthouse next to the line. Note: if this chart for your own use, you can eliminate the M after the bearing to avoid cluttering the chart more than you have to.

Realign the rule over the 110-degree mark on the compass rose and roll it down over the center of the Shark Island Lighthouse, repeating the previous procedure.

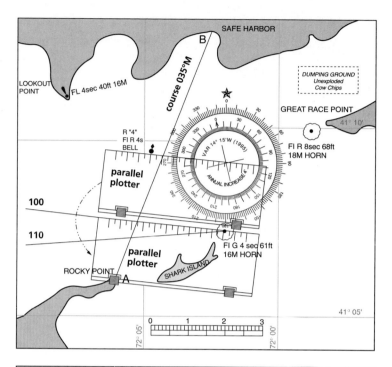

Continue repeating the above steps at 10-degree increments.

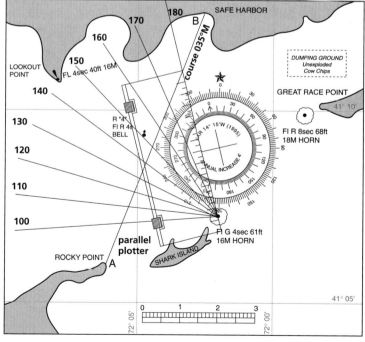

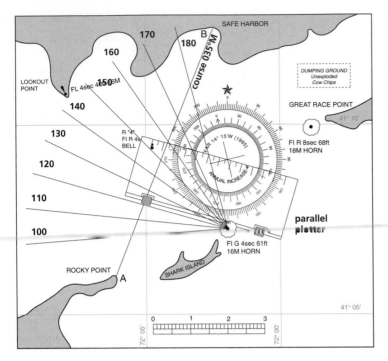

Next, align the rule over the center of the rose and the 120-degree mark on the magnetic compass scale.

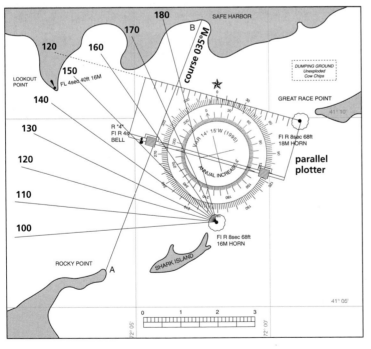

Transfer the bearing line to the center of the Great Race Lighthouse as you did previously. It is a good idea to use different color pencils to differentiate the bearings of each lighthouse.

Repeat the procedure until the chart appears similar to the illustration.

BELOW RIGHT: Armed with your pre-navigation chart, you are now well into your trip. You've been paddling for a while, and you want to check on your position. Turning your kayak to face the Great Race Lighthouse or taking a bearing with your handheld compass, you notice the compass reads 95 degrees. You then check your position relative to the Shark Island Lighthouse, and the compass reads 135 degrees.

Looking down at your chart, you mentally place your position fix where the kayak is shown in the illustration. If conditions are not too bad, you may want to mark your position along with the time.

According to this fix, you see that wind or current has pushed you well to the west of your course. If you had read the current tables or considered the wind, you could have compensated for it and been closer to your intended course.

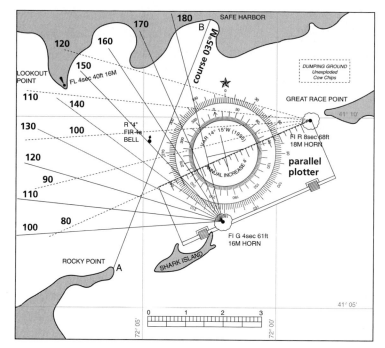

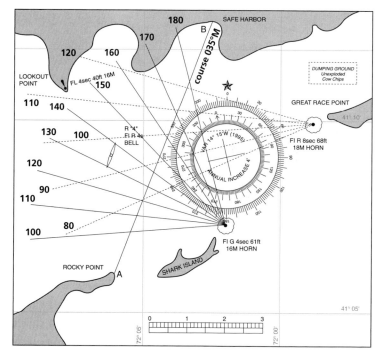

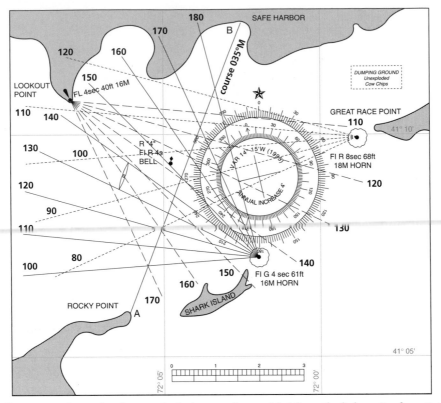

The illustration shows the chart with the bearing lines added from the light at Lookout Point (drawn in a third pattern to distinguish them). Using this third line of sight, you more accurately fix your position. The chart indicates your kayak is at a bearing of 160 degrees from Lookout Point Light.

You've now triangulated your position (i.e., fixed it with three bearings). The intersection of the bearing from Lookout Point should be quite close to the intersection of the other two bearings, so you know your position to a fairly high degree of accuracy.

There are a number of other tools you can use to make your life simpler as a navigator, such as plastic grids with the variation lines already printed on them. Some are manufactured, but many are handmade (see Chapter 9). As you go along in your quest for learning, you will become familiar with other tools. You should only use them, however, after you understand the fundamental principles of navigation. It is similar to learning how to do basic arithmetic before getting a calculator. Possibly the most sophisticated and expensive of these tools is the Global Positioning System (GPS). Many people are already using these units out on the water. The next chapter will discuss using a GPS unit as it relates to kayak navigation.

9 Navigating with GPS

THE GLOBAL POSITIONING SYSTEM (GPS) WAS developed by the Department of Defense and became available to civilians in the 1980s. It is a network of 24 active satellites orbiting the Earth twice a day, transmitting signals that a GPS receiver uses to triangulate position. With a good signal, a GPS receiver can provide you with an accurate horizontal location (i.e., latitude and longitude) to within 30–50 feet. The vertical elevation obtained by using only satellite signals is not quite as accurate, but since you're on flat water you won't need this information. Besides, unless you're on an inland lake or river, you already know your elevation: sea level.

> The illiterate of the future will not be the person who cannot read. It will be the person who does not know how to learn.
>
> GEORGE F. WILL

New GPS receivers are even more accurate because of the Wide Area Augmentation System (WAAS). WAAS is a system of satellites and ground stations that provides GPS signal corrections. Corrections are necessary because various factors affect GPS accuracy (e.g., ionospheric interferences, signal reflection, and satellite position). A GPS receiver that is WAAS enabled will be accurate to less than 10 feet, 95 percent of the time (which is pretty darn good in my view).

Currently WAAS coverage is limited to the continental United States, Alaska, some of Southern Canada, and parts of Northern Mexico. To enable your receiver to receive WAAS signals, you'll need to turn on the feature in the setup menu. However, keep in mind that if you are in an area that does not support WAAS, you must turn the feature off so you don't get false readings.

Although the coordinates given by the GPS are very accurate, the software charts purchased with a GPS unit may not be. For example, during a recent trip on New Jersey's Barnegat Bay in a friend's powerboat, the GPS screen showed that we were traveling directly through an island. The receiver was indicating accuracy to about 9 feet at the time. So what happened?

The chart on the GPS showed 2 small sedge islands, one about 2,500 feet long and the other perhaps 500 feet long. The paper chart showed the same islands. But because we paddled this area often, we knew the islands had changed over the years. The smaller one was now completely gone, and the larger island was less than a third of its charted size. Digital charting software used in GPS receivers is derived from paper charts. Because the sea is a dynamic area, things change, and it takes a while for charts to be updated. This is especially true for areas that do not command great importance to navigators.

Newer GPS receivers come with such a plethora of features, with many of them having little to do with basic navigation, that they deserve a book by themselves. And as you might surmise, there are many good books out there (a few of which are listed in Appendix A). To complicate matters, GPS receivers have different levels of features and different menu systems. Higher-priced units are able to do more than inexpensive units. So how did I distill all this information down to one chapter? The answer is "I didn't."

Rather, I decided to keep this topic simple and only discuss the very basic functions you can perform with a GPS that will allow you to navigate your kayak. I own a Garmin 76CS, which has 115 megabytes of memory and allows the loading of optional road maps, topographical maps, and charts. All of the specific instructions and photos in this chapter refer to this unit. So where I mention certain buttons to press or menus to view, keep in mind that your unit may be different (although probably quite similar). Other similar, popular brands include Magellan and Lowrance.

To navigate with a GPS, you still need to understand basic navigation and know how to read charts. Sorry—I know what you were wishing.

The photo at right shows two GPS receivers. The one on the right is an older unit that does not have any mapping capabilities. You will also notice it has an antenna that rotates up for use. Although it is not as fancy as the newer receivers, it still is very useful for navigating.

The unit on the left has the antenna inside the unit under the globe symbol. This unit should be held horizontally for optimum reception. The screen shows the opening page and indicates how many satellites the unit is able to view and from which it can obtain signals.

GPS receivers.

LET'S GET STARTED

With GPSs coming down in price and getting more features, we are seeing the technology everywhere—cars, boats, and planes. They are being used by hikers, bikers, fishermen, hunters, kayakers, and anyone else who wants to pinpoint their location or get directions to a destination. Applications vary. Municipalities use GPSs to pinpoint sewer manholes, locate underground utilities, power lines, and so on. Law enforcement authorities use them to track the location of criminals on probation. There is even a game, or sport, called geocaching, in which someone hides an item and posts the coordinates on the web; other GPS users race to be the first one to find it. Although the system and technology are extremely complex, the GPS units are actually quite easy to use.

Let's begin our discussion with a few definitions:

- Waypoint. The latitude and longitude coordinates of a particular location. You can store multiple waypoints in the memory of your GPS receiver and navigate to them. For instance, you could create a waypoint for a buoy, a beach, or even the parking lot where you left your car. With the waypoints stored, the GPS receiver can help you find their physical locations.
- Route. A series of waypoints entered into the receiver. For instance, you could connect the waypoints from your parked car, to the buoy, to the beach as a route. The GPS receiver can then help you navigate along that route to the beach and back.
- Track. When activated, the tracking feature will automatically store a series of points that indicate your actual travel path. This is sort of like a digital trail of breadcrumbs.

GPS receivers are computers. A GPS receiver takes basic coded signal information from dedicated satellites and provides the coordinates of your location. If you are in motion, the GPS receiver will constantly update your coordinates in real-time, and provide your speed over ground, and your direction. If you are following a course to a waypoint, the GPS will provide you with your speed made good, and give you an estimated time of arrival.

Many of the newer GPS receivers come equipped with a simple map—called a base map—that may show major roads, cities, and waterways. Usually, there is not a great deal of detail in these maps. You can buy supplemental maps that overlay more details onto the base map. In addition, these units may come with software. Once installed, the software will allow you to save waypoints and make routes on your home computer then upload that information to the GPS receiver.

WHAT DO I GET FOR MY MONEY?

Today, GPS receivers range in price from about $100 to $600. Which receiver to purchase will depend upon how much money you want to spend and what features are important to you. It's similar to buying a car. There will be some features you want that you'll only find in the higher-priced units, but at the same time, you'll also be paying for features you may not need or want. Size is also important. Some types of receivers are made for use in vehicles or larger boats, and these will be too large for the deck of a kayak. Also, many of these receivers are not waterproof. For obvious reasons, you'll want to get a handheld, waterproof unit.

Ah, but which one?

A basic receiver gives current LatLon coordinates and allows you to view your speed, distance, and direction to your destination. They store 250 or more waypoints and a number of routes. They may remember up to 10 track logs, as well as give the time of sunrise and sunset. Most will track up to 12 satellites and have about 8 MB of memory. These inexpensive units usually do not have internal base maps. Some are waterproof.

A mid-priced unit does everything above and also stores more waypoints, track logs, and routes. Most units in this price range contain a base map, usually in grayscale. (Once you see how little detail there is on a base map, you may elect to buy a higher-priced model.) These receivers may have a small amount of memory, perhaps as little as 8 MB, although some range from 24–56 MB. Some units allow loading of additional cartography, but the coverage area may be limited by the receiver's available memory. Adding more detailed maps or charts involves extra costs. In my case, I purchased from the GPS manufacturer a CD containing charts of most of the Americas. When I paid for the CD, I received one unlock code that allowed me load a particular range of charts to my GPS receiver. I loaded charts from New York to Delaware; however, if I wanted to load charts from a different region, I would have to purchase another unlock code. The mapping programs are usually proprietary and quite expensive.

As you may guess, high-priced receivers do even more. They come with an internal base map and have a 256-color screen that shows up very well, even in sunlight. They may have a substantial amount of memory (115 MB), which means you can download and store maps that display in color, topos, or charts of different areas.

Some higher-end units predict the tides in different areas. Many units have built-in altimeters (based on barometric pressure) and electronic compasses. Other features may include sun and moon times and phases, an alarm clock, stopwatch, calendar, calculator, and games. And all units, both inexpensive and costly, display extremely accurate time since they obtain it from the satellites' atomic clocks.

Many GPS units are rated as waterproof to IEC 60529 IPX-7 standards: submersible to 1 meter for up to 30 minutes. Some units even float. However, take note: *waterproof* isn't as definitive a term as you might think. Back in 1997 I owned a GPS receiver that was purported to be waterproof. I was using it while paddling on Florida Bay; no waves splashed on it, and it did not fall in. It was, however, exposed to some water from paddle drips. The next day, there was a green slime on the inside of the display, and the unit would not work. When I got home, I called the manufacturer about it. They told me that I should have brought their other model because it was "more waterproof." I said, "I don't understand. How can something be more waterproof? Either it's waterproof or it's not." The reply was "Well, that's the marketing people for you." I eventually bought a different brand and kept it in a plastic waterproof case for years, which made it harder to work the buttons and view the screen. The one I have now seems to be holding to its waterproof claims— so far. You'll need to determine for yourself if yours really is waterproof.

If you purchase a GPS that is supposed to float, test it. If you have a waterproof unit that does not float, you need to put it in a float bag or at least tie a lanyard to it, so when you drop it you don't have to watch it sink. (Also be sure you can read the unit in sunlight before you buy it.)

GETTING TO KNOW YOUR GPS RECEIVER

If you've purchased your first GPS receiver, congratulations! But before you start using your new toy, get to know it. Read the manual—yes, men, this means you— and become familiar with your unit's menu system and features. The following photos show the various buttons and some of the screens (pages) of a typical GPS unit. Because receivers do differ, some may have one button serving two functions, or a function may be in a menu.

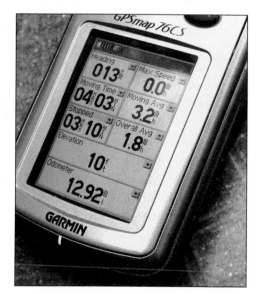

The photo at right shows the unit with the trip computer page visible. This page displays your heading, maximum speed, moving time, moving average, stopped time, overall average, elevation, and odometer. With this unit, you can remove or replace these data fields for other fields that relate more to how you use the unit. For example, you may prefer to have the current time showing rather than the time you were stopped. The list of choices is long.

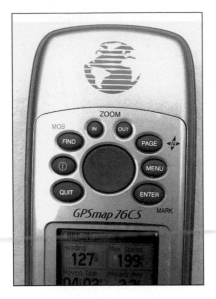

This photo shows a close-up of the control buttons on a GPS receiver. Starting with the center button, then reading clockwise, the buttons and their functions are listed below:

- **Center rocker**. Pressing this button at the quadrants allows you to scroll through and highlight different areas of the screen boxes. You can go up, down, left, and right. On the map page, you can use this button to pan to a different part of the map.
- **Quit**. This button can be used to delete erroneous data entry. It can also be used to switch the screen back to a previous page.
- **Power/Backlight**. Aside from turning the unit on and off, this button—when pressed quickly—turns on the backlight for easy reading at nighttime. To conserve the battery, the backlight can be programmed to turn off after a set time has elapsed.
- **Find/MOB (man overboard)**. By pressing and releasing this button, you can search for previously entered waypoints, routes, or tracks. Holding the button longer instantly marks the coordinates of your current position; this is known as the man overboard button, or MOB. For instance, suppose someone fell overboard from a larger ship. Pushing the MOB button marks the coordinates where the person went into the water. After the captain has the boat turned around, he can return to that exact spot. As a kayaker, you might use this function if you drop an item into shallow water at high tide. Then you could go back to that exact spot at low tide to look for it. (Of course, in reality, you'll never find that watch—don't ask me how I know.)
- **Zoom In/Out**. These buttons provide either a closer or broader view of the map page.
- **Page**. Every time this button is pressed, a different screen is displayed. Some units allow you to arrange the particular pages you want to view. For instance, if your unit has an altimeter, and you only use the GPS for kayaking, you may not want to view the elevation page since you will always be at or near sea level if paddling on the coast. Holding the Page button down longer turns the electronic compass on and off.
- **Menu**. This button opens the main menu or the menu for the particular page you are viewing. Each page has its own set of menus.
- **Enter/Mark**. This button opens a set of options for a page, or it is used to select an option. When held down, it will copy a waypoint into memory and automatically assign an identification name such as 001, 002, or 003. You'll have the option to rename the waypoint as something more meaningful or memorable. Once you've entered this information, remember to save it.

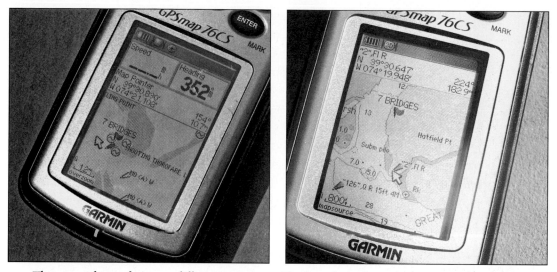

These two photos show two different map pages. The first photo shows the base map that came with the GPS. Notice where it says "7 Bridges"? This is a waypoint I entered; it is a local put-in to go out to the inlet. The second photo shows a chart covering the same area but in greater detail. This is from a chart that I purchased separately and loaded onto the GPS receiver. You can see how much more it looks like a paper chart, giving depth soundings, contours, and additional buoy information.

If I find myself at the entrance to the inlet, especially in fog or at night, I can press the Find button, scroll to "7 Bridges," hit Enter, and use the GoTo option, which will lead me directly to "7 Bridges." Of course, a GPS unit will not always know if an island is between you and your destination, and it won't tell you that a boat is bearing down on you. You still need an up-to-date chart of the area, your five senses, and good judgment.

Electronic Compass

The electronic compass works the same as a nonelectronic compass—that is, by detecting the Earth's magnetic field. It must be kept level when being used. If

RIGHT: *This photo shows the menu page. To access the different choices, use the rocker button to scroll to the item you want, press Enter, and you'll get a set of options.*

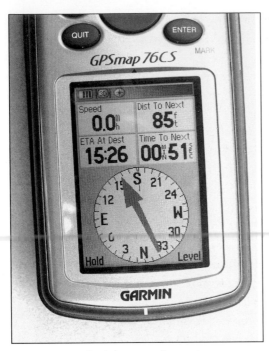

GPS receiver displaying an electronic compass.

you want to conserve battery power, turn on the compass only when you need it. You can turn it on or off through the menu.

Not all units have a built-in electronic compass, and one isn't absolutely necessary because a GPS unit can still show direction—just not as conveniently. A normal GPS receiver detects direction as a function of movement. The satellites tell the unit where it was a few moments ago and where it is now, so it can calculate the direction. However, when you stop, the receiver no longer detects movement and so cannot determine direction. Even with a GPS unit, it is a good idea to always have a regular magnetic compass along.

To save battery power, you can set a compass-equipped GPS to activate the compass only when the unit is moving at a certain speed for a certain amount of time. I have mine set so that if I am going faster than 1 knot for more than 15 seconds, it will switch input from the electronic compass and use the satellites to determine my direction.

Because I had entered a destination waypoint, the accompanying photo shows an arrow that rotates independently of the electronic compass. To get to my desired location, I only need to turn my kayak so the red arrow points directly toward the top of the receiver. In the example shown in the photo, I have to turn to my left to stay on course.

First Time Out

Before turning on the unit, put in fresh batteries. Most units can use regular or rechargeable batteries. Buying rechargeable batteries and a charger may save some money if you use it a lot. You may want to try both types and see how long each type lasts.

The first page that will come up will read something like "Locating satellites," then "Acquiring satellites." The first time the receiver is powered up, the unit may take a long time to find itself. Keep in mind, it may have been made a far distance from where it is now, and it has no idea in which part of the world it currently resides. You can shorten this searching time by going to "New Location" from the menu and tell it the area of the world it is in. The next time you turn on the unit, it will find the satellites far more quickly.

To receive the signal, a unit needs a clear view of the sky. If you are in a heavily wooded area or a city with tall buildings, your GPS unit may not be able to lock on to the satellites. You can explore and practice with it indoors by using the demo mode. At the Main Menu, you should see a Setup icon. Scroll to it and hit Enter. Now look for the System icon. Scroll to it and press Enter. On this unit, there are a number of boxes, each with its own option. The top box on my unit is labeled "GPS," and the options are Normal, Battery Saver, GPS Off, and Demo Mode. If you select Demo Mode, the receiver is shut off and does not try to locate the satellites or acquire signals. While in this mode, you can enter waypoints, view menus, change options, and so on. The next time you power up, it will revert back to Normal to keep you from trying to navigate with false readings.

Some other GPS menu settings that are likely to be used for kayaking are discussed below.

Map Datum

Since the Earth is not perfectly round and has mountains and valleys, there has to be a standard so that accurate calculations can be performed. A map datum, which is nothing more than a mathematical model of the Earth's surface, fills this need. There are a large number of different map datums in use. Most current charts use the World Geodetic Survey of 1984 (WGS 84). However, you should check your maps, charts, or topos to see what datum they are using and set your unit to agree with it. The topo maps I have show the 1927 North American datum (NAD 27) on them.

Grid System

If using a chart, set your receiver to Latitude/Longitude since all charts will have a LatLon grid on it. If you decide to use U.S. Geological Survey maps (topos), you will see they have a Universal Transverse Mercator (UTM) grid as well as a latitude/longitude grid; you can set your GPS to either. If you are using LatLon for the topo, you will probably do well to add intermediate lines on the paper map. The topos have marks only at 2½-minute intervals. This means that if the lower latitude mark is 39° 30′, the next mark will be at 39° 32′ 30″ and the following will be at 39° 35′. The one on the top of the map will be 39° 37′ 30″. You will want to interpolate where the 31′, 32′, 33′, 34′, 36′, and 37′ latitude lines are and draw them on the map. Do the same for the longitude lines.

MAKING A GPS OVERLAY GRID

You should make your grid to suit your chart. The grid in the illustration below is divided into 10 parts. If you made a grid for a chart with 1-minute increments, then divided it into 10 parts, each line would represent $^1/_{10}$ of a minute. As a bonus, the horizontal lines can be used as a scale because they are divisions of latitude.

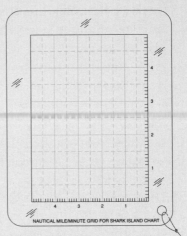

1. Cut a piece of plastic from a sheet protector (sold in office supply stores), making it slightly larger than a rectangle formed by the latitude and longitude lines on your chart.
2. Draw the box formed by the LatLon lines.
3. Divide the latitude and longitude lines into 5 equal parts to get 1-minute increments (since they were 5 minutes apart on this chart). Using a fine tip permanent marking pen, draw these lines on the grid and number them.
4. Divide each 1-minute increment into 10 equal parts and mark short lines on the side and bottom.
5. Draw a dashed line at each $^5/_{10}$ mark to indicate $^1/_2$ minute.
6. Since latitude increases northerly in the northern hemisphere and longitude increases westerly in the western hemisphere, number the lines as appropriate starting from the bottom right.
7. Attach a string to the grid to secure it to a deck line.

NAUTICAL MILE/MINUTE GRID FOR SHARK ISLAND CHART

A grid can help you get a more accurate fix by dividing up the distance between latitude and longitude lines.

North Settings

Set the GPS to the magnetic north option because your deck compass points toward magnetic north.

Distance/Speed

Set distance/speed to nautical miles when using marine charts to correlate the distance and speed with the chart's scale.

Position Format

Set the unit to display coordinate information in this format: *hddd° mm.mmm'*, or degrees, minutes, and tenths of a minute. This is the way charts are set up. Now the GPS-derived coordinates can be plotted on a chart, and chart-derived coordinates can be entered into the GPS. We'll discuss how to do this in the next section.

DETERMINING COORDINATES

As you paddle around, your GPS receiver is constantly spitting out updated coordinates. "That's great," you say. "What do I do with them?" Well, let's say you're in thick fog and you need to know your exact location. You can't take bearing from charted objects because the visibility is too diminished, and your dead reckoned position is just not accurate enough for your present needs. And, to make things that much trickier, let's say your GPS doesn't have built-in charts. In this case, you would need to transfer the coordinates from your GPS to your chart. How do we do this? The most common tool for this is a pair of dividers, but they're sharp, ungainly, and only truly effective when you're able to spread out your entire chart over a large, flat surface. For this reason, many people make a grid on clear plastic to divide the distance between the latitude and longitude lines into smaller increments (see the sidebar). Charts may show LatLon lines as increments of 1, 2, or 5 minutes depending on the scale of the chart, and smaller divisions may appear only on the chart's margins (see the photograph on page 13). A plastic grid, however, will help you extend those lines into the body of the chart.

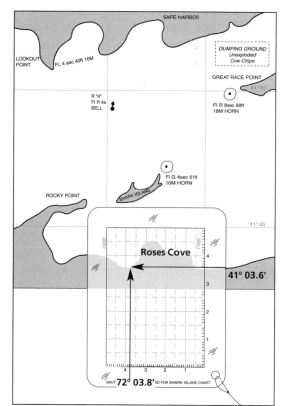

The plastic grid can be used in reverse, too. Let's say you want to input a destination—Roses Cove, for instance—into your GPS receiver as a waypoint. The accompanying figure shows how to determine the coordinates. Place the grid tool over the chart, and align the horizontal and vertical lines with the LatLon lines. The closest latitude to Roses Cove is 41° 05´. Since the solid lines on the plastic grid represent 1 minute, we know that the bottom of the grid is at 41°00´. Counting up to Roses Cove, we see it is more than 03´ but less than 04´. We count up the small (tenths) division marks and get 6 tenths above 03´. Therefore the latitude is 41° 03.6´. Following the same procedure to determine the longitude gives us 72° 03.8´. Now you can enter

You can determine coordinates from a chart by using a plastic grid.

the coordinates 41° 03.6′ N 72° 03.8′ W into your GPS receiver, and set up Roses Cove as a waypoint.

SO, HOW DO I USE MY GPS?

There are three basic ways to navigate using a GPS, all of which are best done in conjunction with a chart:

1. **GoTo.** A straight path to a waypoint. Depending upon the features your unit has, you can enter the waypoint in one of several ways:

- By scrolling to the desired location on the GPS's map page and entering it.
- By using a clear plastic grid (as described previously) to get the intermediate minutes and tenths of a minute then entering the new waypoint's coordinates manually.
- With some mapping programs you can enter waypoints into your home computer and download them to your GPS.
- If you are currently at a location that you would like to store as a waypoint for future reference, all you need to do is press a single button (consult your owner's manual). The waypoint will automatically be given a name, which you can then rename to something more suitable.

2. **Tracks.** If the tracking feature is turned on, the GPS will collect data points during your wanderings that you can later display on the screen. Sort of like a breadcrumb trail. This track can be configured to record the data at set intervals of either time or distance. At each interval, the GPS records your location and the time. If you are traveling a route that has long straight runs, you can set the unit to capture data at every $1/4$ or $1/2$ mile or so. Conversely, if you are paddling through a myriad of turns, say going through a marshy area with many different paths, you can set it for much shorter distances, although this will use up more memory. After you reach your destination, the GPS unit can use this track to guide you back the way you came. You can store these tracks in the GPS memory bank for future trips.

3. **Routes.** A series of waypoints that will get you from point A to point B when there is no direct path. These waypoints can be pre-entered or entered en route at every turn or intersection. As with tracking, you can both reverse the route and save it as well.

Are you ready for some examples?

GoTo

As illustrated below, you are aimlessly wandering along the coast, away from shore, and finally decide to turn around and go back. Wow, you're 5 miles away. You look at where you came from and can't figure out where your car is. The whole coast looks the same. Not to worry. Roses Cove was your launch spot, and you'd entered it as a waypoint earlier.

To return to your car, press the Find button, scroll to the waypoint for Roses Cove, choose the GoTo function, and let the unit guide you back. (If your unit has a specific GoTo button, press that first then select the waypoint).

Tracking

Suppose you want to explore a group of closely spaced islands; however, there are so many islands that you have concerns you may not find your way back in time before night falls. This is where the tracking feature comes in handy. Before you start out, turn the tracking feature on and set the recording time or distance to an appropriate interval. When you have completed your exploration, set the receiver to backtrack and you'll be guided right back the way you came. If instead, you tried to use the GoTo function to find your way back to the launch site, you'd be in for a bumpy paddle. (See the illustrations on the following page.)

Routes

Another way for you to navigate with a GPS is by using the Routes function. You might use this method for a longer distance trip, where you have more straight lines of travel between changes in direction. You may periodically turn off the unit when used this way. Although you could use tracking, if your trip is a long one, the tracking function would record a lot of data points and use up more memory. You may also run out of battery power because you would have to keep your unit on for a long time. (One should be wary of putting in new batter-

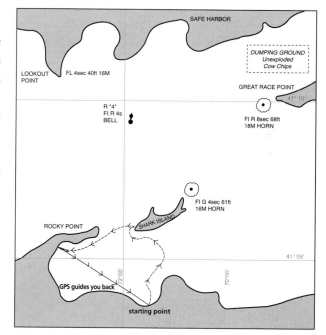

Using the GoTo function to return home.

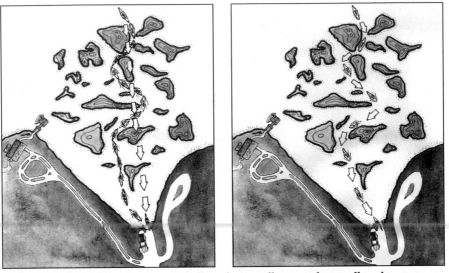

going
out

coming
home

LEFT: *Using the GoTo function to return to your launch site will not work so well in this situation.* RIGHT: *Instead, the tracking feature will guide you back along your original path through the islands.*

ies while out on the water. Wet hands, splashing, or a wave may get water in the unit and ruin it.)

While at home or another convenient place, turn on the receiver and set waypoints for your launch site, your final destination, and any changes in direction in between. For instance, you may want to enter as waypoints the location of any buoys that may be along your route. You may be more comfortable paddling to intermediate points along your route than in a straight line to your destination, using the buoys as confirmation that you're still on course. If you have the charts loaded on your unit, you can use the center rocker to pan over to a buoy. If your software shows the LatLon for the buoy, hit Enter to mark it as a waypoint. If you need to enter the coordinates manually, use the plastic grid as described previously. The top two illustrations on the facing page depict the use of a plastic grid to obtain the coordinates of the buoys and the destination.

Once you've entered all the waypoints, save the route and name it something logical or memorable.

If you own a GPS that can load charts, you may be able to use your home computer to create your route then upload it to the GPS. Utilizing the computer's keyboard and mouse for this task—especially renaming waypoints—is easier than fumbling with the thumb pads on the GPS receiver itself.

So, the route has been planned and saved in your GPS receiver and now you're

114

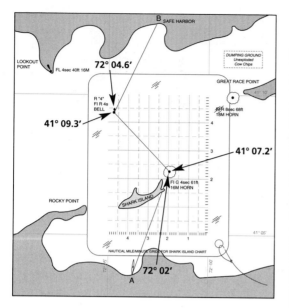

Use a grid to determine the coordinates to plug into your Routes function. Here it is used to determine coordinates for these buoys . . .

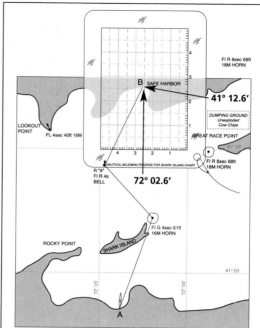

. . . and here for the route destination.

out paddling it. What's next? Well, you can let the GPS receiver guide you along your route much like the tracking feature returned you to your launch site in the previous example; however, you'll draw a lot of power from your batteries if you keep it on during your entire trip, so it might be best to check it periodically to confirm your position or to get bearings to your next waypoint.

You can also use the GPS to determine if wind or currents are pushing you in a particular direction and at what speed. To find out, stop paddling for a

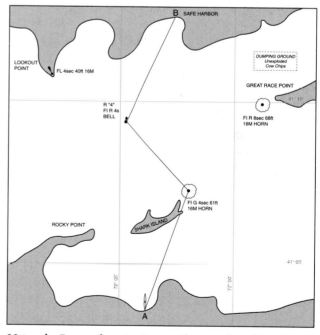

Using the Routes function is a good option for a long trip.

115

minute or so and check the speed over ground and direction displays. Then turn it off again and continue with your trip. If your GPS indicated that you were being pushed to the left, compensate by aiming off course to the right.

SECURING YOUR GPS

After purchasing a GPS unit, you don't want to lose it overboard, so securing it is important. Many kayakers secure their GPS units under a deck bungee. While a solution, this location may make it hard

Hold on to your GPS receiver by attaching it to straps sewn to the sprayskirt.

to see the unit. I suggest sewing narrow elastic straps on the front of the sprayskirt and securing the unit to these. The straps will prevent the GPS unit from being swept away. Depending upon the type of elastic cord or strap you use, one band may be adequate to hold it on, and it will certainly make it easier to take out when you need it. As an extra precaution, you can use a lanyard to attach the GPS to the sprayskirt grab loop or to your PFD. (Do not fasten the lanyard to a deck bungee or perimeter line because it may interfere with the release of the sprayskirt in a wet exit.)

Although you can purchase mounting brackets that fit a GPS unit, they are best used on automobiles or larger boats. However, if you really want to mount the GPS on a kayak, drill some holes into the deck and secure the bracket with stainless steel screws and a backing plate. You will need to mount the GPS close to the cockpit in order to reach the buttons. Keep in mind that this location can interfere with rescues. At the very least, dragging boats and bodies over the deck during rescues may break the unit.

FINAL NOTE

Although a GPS receiver has many applications and benefits, it has some shortcomings. Batteries can die, the unit can break, or it can go overboard. A GPS doesn't negate the need to know how to navigate—a prudent paddler will understand the basic principles of navigation and be prepared for any eventuality.

Epilogue

NOW THAT WE HAVE COMPLETED OUR NAVIGATION OF THIS BOOK, LET'S think about our journey. Some readers may have started out already knowing much of this material; others perhaps knowing little. I hope everyone has learned something from it.

We started out with an introduction to navigation, then moved on to the difference between magnetic north and true north, how to use charts, latitude and longitude, and aids to navigation. We discussed how to use the compass and compass rose to determine our course and take bearings and how tides and currents affect us. We learned how to estimate speed and use ranges to keep on course and discussed some examples of how to compensate for current. We also learned to do a simple ferry angle calculation and to prepare a chart to help us easily determine our position using landmarks, without having to draw on the chart while our kayak is bouncing in the waves. We ended our journey by learning what a GPS receiver can do to augment navigation.

If you wish to continue learning about navigation, I refer you to Further Reading in Appendix A. Here you'll find resources from which you can learn about celestial navigation; electronic navigation (such as radar and radio navigation systems); and harbor, coastal, and even ocean crossings using wind patterns and ocean currents. For those interested in learning more about navigating with GPS, there are books that go into far more detail than can be covered in one chapter.

There is a plethora of information on buoys, rules of the road, night navigation, and so on, that will certainly aid you as a kayaker. There are also other methods and navigation aids that will help you accomplish what we have covered in this book; some of which may work better for you.

Many advanced navigation methods have limited use for kayakers. We tend to do much shorter trips and have little space to carry extra equipment. What this book has given you is the basic navigation principles to get you safely there and back, but only if you practice them.

Safety includes other aspects of kayaking that are essential. I urge you to gather as much information as you can on all facets of the sport. Take a kayaking course *from a qualified instructor,* such as one certified by the American Canoe Association, to learn paddling skills. Learn and practice various rescues so they become intuitive and can be performed quickly. Take a rolling class to learn to right your kayak in the event of a capsize. Wear a PFD and appropriate clothing. Get to know and fully understand the marine environment.

This is an exciting time for sea kayaking. As of this printing, it is one of the fastest growing sports. With this surge in popularity comes a host of enthusiastic new paddlers eager to get out and kayak, sometimes getting into situations for which they do not yet have the skills or experience to cope.

I have always maintained that sea kayaking is a very, very safe sport that can get dangerous very quickly if one does not have the proper skills, knowledge, or judgment. Work to develop all three, and your paddling will be safe and enjoyable.

Glossary

aids to navigation (atons): Anything (not on a vessel) used to aid in navigation, e.g., buoys and lights

bearing: The direction of an object, expressed either as a true bearing or magnetic bearing, as shown on the chart or as a bearing relative to the heading of the boat

bow: The forward part of a boat

buoy: An anchored float used for marking a position on the water, a hazard or a shoal; also used for mooring

chart: A map used by navigators

compass: A device to determine direction using the Earth's magnetic field

compass rose: An imprinted circular scale used on a chart to display true north and magnetic north for that particular chart

course: The direction you want to head

current: The horizontal movement of the water

daymark: An aid to navigation used in shallow water and similar to a buoy, except that it is a permanently fixed structure rather than an anchored and floating one. Also called a daybeacon.

dead reckoning (DR): A method of navigation used when an accurate fix cannot be obtained. Your position at sea is determined by applying direction, speed, and time traveled to the last known fix.

degree: A unit of angular measure equaling $1/360$ of a circle

deviation: A false reading from the compass caused by items such as iron or steel, as well as electric circuits

diurnal tide: One high water level and one low water level occur in approximately 24 hours

drift: The speed at which the current moves; measured in knots

ebb tide: A falling or receding tide

estimated position (EP): A probable position. It is usually a DR position modified to account for current and wind drift.

ferry angle calculation: A vector solution to determine the proper heading to take to compensate for current

ferrying: The act of pointing the bow up current or upwind to offset the effects of the current or wind

fix: Establishing your position using the intersection of two or more lines of position or by passing closely to an object of which you know the location. A fix that is based on two lines of position is not as accurate as one based on three.

flood tide: A rising tide

following sea: An overtaking sea that comes from astern

GPS: Global Positioning System

GPS receiver: An electronic instrument that receives satellite signals to determine a position anywhere on the Earth

heading: The direction in which a vessel's bow points at any given time

high tide: Highest level attained by an incoming tide

knot: A measure of speed equal to 1 nautical mile per hour

latitude: The imaginary lines running parallel to the equator

LatLon: Denotes latitude and longitude. Latitude always given first.

lighthouse: A tower or lofty structure with a light at the top to serve as a guide or warning to ships at night

line of position (LOP): A line drawn on the chart from an object at a bearing, or a range, which corresponds to your line of sight to that object

longitude: The imaginary lines running from the north pole to the south pole

low tide: Lowest level attained by an outgoing tide

mean high water (MHW): Average height of all high waters at a specific place over a 19-year cycle

mean higher high water (MHHW): Average height of all higher high waters at a specific place over a 19-year cycle

mean low water (MLW): Average height of all low waters at a specific place over a 19-year cycle

mean lower low water (MLLW): Average height of all lower low waters at a specific place over a 19-year cycle

meridian: See "longitude"

minute: As pertains to navigation, $1/60$ of a degree

nautical mile: One minute of latitude; approximately 6,076 feet. It is equal to 1.15 (about $1 1/8$) statute miles.

navigation: The art and science of conducting a boat safely from one point to another

navigational aid: Anything on a vessel used to aid in navigation, e.g., charts and compasses

neap tide: A tide in which there is the least amount of difference between the high and low tides (range of tide). It occurs during the first and last quarters of the moon, when the Earth, sun, and moon form a right angle.

pile: A wood, metal, or concrete pole driven into the sea bottom

piloting: Navigation by use of visible references

port: The left side of a boat when looking forward

range: Any two natural or man-made objects that appear in line from your perspective

range of tide: Difference between high and low water levels

route: A series of directions to get from point A to point B. In GPS terms, it is a series of linked waypoints entered into the receiver.

second: As it pertains to navigation, $\frac{1}{60}$ of a minute

semi-diurnal tide: Two high water levels and two low water levels occur in approximately 24 hours

set: The direction in which a current flows

SMG: Speed made good over ground; also known as VMG (velocity made good)

spring tide: A tide that has the greatest difference between high and low tides (range of tide). It occurs during the full and new moons, when the sun, moon, and Earth are aligned.

starboard: The right side of a boat when looking forward

stern: The rear of a boat

statute mile: A measure of distance used on land; 5,280 feet or 0.87 nautical mile

tide: The periodic rise and fall of the water level in the ocean

tidal race: A region of very turbulent water occurring when a fast current passes over an irregular sea floor or when opposing currents meet. Also known as tide rips or rips.

track: A series of points stored in a GPS receiver that indicate your travel path

variation: The angle at which magnetic north varies from true north

waypoint: The latitude and longitude coordinates of a particular location. You can store them in memory on your GPS and navigate to them.

Further Reading

Check bookstores or online retailers for these excellent titles.

NAVIGATION-SPECIFIC BOOKS

Fundamentals of Kayak Navigation
David Burch
ISBN 1-56440-155-3

Sea Kayak Navigation
Franco Ferrero
ISBN 0-9531956-1-9

The Navigator's Handbook
Jeff Toghill
ISBN 1-58574-791-2

BOOKS WITH CHAPTERS ON NAVIGATION

The Complete Sea Kayaker's Handbook
Shelley Johnson
ISBN: 0-07-136210-X

Sea Kayaking Illustrated
John Robison
ISBN: 0-07-139234-3

The Complete Book of Sea Kayaking, **Fourth Edition**
Derek C. Hutchinson
ISBN 1-56440-722-5

Sea Kayaker's *Savvy Paddler*
Doug Alderson
ISBN: 0-07-136203-7

Sea Kayaking
Nigel Foster
ISBN 0-906754-60-7

Sea Kayaker *Magazine's Handbook of Safety and Rescue*
Doug Alderson and Michael Pardy
ISBN: 0-07-138890-7

The Essential Sea Kayaker
David Seidman
ISBN: 0-07-136237-1

The Complete Guide to Sea Kayak Touring, **Second Edition**
Jonathan Hanson
ISBN: 0-07-026204-7

GPS-SPECIFIC BOOKS

GPS for Mariners
Robert J. Sweet
ISBN 0-07-141075-9

GPS Made Easy
Lawrence Letham
ISBN 0-89886-823-8

Online Navigation Resources

*Compiled by Timothy Williams, ACA Coastal Kayaking Instructor**

T HIS SECTION WILL PROVIDE A MAP OF SORTS FOR THOSE WISHING MORE information on navigation. Equipment, planning resources, and raw data are referenced here for your benefit.

The Internet has opened a new world of data to the lay person, and for proper trip planning using the methods described in this book, the Internet can be quite useful. Information on tides, currents, and weather conditions and prediction all may be accessed through online resources. The World Wide Web began as a tool to help researchers and academics communicate and share information. Although sometimes forgotten, this use is still possible.

A note of caution is required, though. When using online resources and information, the source is quite important. It is necessary for the user of online data to verify the source and, if possible, the accuracy of any data obtained. An "honest mistake" made by a web author or designer in navigational calculation or information may challenge the patience, abilities, or life of the unwary user. Data changes constantly and even government sites are subject to flaws. Double-check all vital information prior to use.

PLANNING

Tide and Current Prediction

National Ocean Service/NOAA Center for Operational Oceanographic Products and Services (CO-OPS)

CO-OPS collects, analyzes, and distributes historical and real-time observations and predictions of water levels, coastal currents, and other meteorological and oceanographic data.

---

* This author makes no endorsement concerning the absolute accuracy of information provided on any website listed. Sites have been chosen based upon their historical dependability and accuracy. This section has been compiled using source material that is in its original form or links easily back to that source. Many of the sites are connected with government agencies or nongovernmental foundations. Listing of commercial sites does not indicate any connection or endorsement, financial or otherwise, of the information or products referenced.

Being a U.S. Government site intended originally for use by research and commercial parties, this information is certified and used as a benchmark for many other programs, calculators, and lists. A wealth of information is available here, including addresses for remote real-time observation stations, warnings to mariners, and severe weather information.

Home: http://co-ops.nos.noaa.gov/index.html

Water level and current predictions:

http://co-ops.nos.noaa.gov/tide_pred.html

X-Tide

This harmonic tide predictor is a free Unix-based software program developed and maintained by David Flater. It provides tide and current predictions and seems to work well in many areas. Graphs and calendars can be generated, and a tide clock installed on the user's desktop. It works with X-series Windows systems, Mac OS, plain text, or the Web. It is continually being upgraded and modified to make it more user friendly. While Mr. Flater has done an excellent job of writing the program and documenting its operational characteristics, he notes that this is not a certified-accurate system. Despite this, once a real-time, in-person evaluation of a tidal area has been made, the X-Tide program may be quite useful. It's most accurate in the United States and Canada but does provide worldwide station data and harmonics.

http://www.flaterco.com/xtide/

Tide Tool 2.2

For the Palm OS, Walter Bilofsky has designed a freeware program, similar in output to X-Tide, for 7,000 locations worldwide. It's been featured in *Sea Kayaker* magazine and includes hundreds of testimonials and endorsements.

http://www.toolworks.com/bilofsky/tidetool/

Tides

This freeware program for Palm OS is compatible with Windows and Mac OS. Designed by Ken Hancock, it is in common use as a portable tide predictor.

http://members.aol.com/khancock/pilot.html#Tides

Nobeltec

This company produces the most popular software for tide and current prediction. *Tides and Currents 3.3* is the latest version and comes with *e-Chart Planner,* a system for route planning and upload-download communication between PC and GPS units. Their product, *Tidal Data*, provides additional tidal prediction sites. Coverage is available worldwide, with modules sold by region.

http://www.nobeltec.com/products/prod_tides.asp

They also provide a nice graphic tide and tidal current predictor at this address: http://www.nobeltec.com/services/tides.asp

CHARTS

On May 2, 2001, the U.S. Coast Guard amended its regulations to permit government vessels to use electronic charting and navigation systems in lieu of paper charts. At home and for trip planning, kayakers are turning to these charts because of their currency, accuracy, and ability to be down- or uploaded to home systems or GPS units for field/water use.

Waterproof paper charts remain the most economical and safest option for kayakers in many cases. For learning the basics of navigation, they are a truly hands-on method that appeals to numerous learning styles. At sea, they are more easily retrieved and are not reliant upon batteries or other sensitive variables. They are also much easier to see—an important feature when navigating.

The National Geospatial Intelligence Agency (NGA)

The NGA handles the information for many navigational requirements of military, commercial, and public users. Go to the NGA main page at http://pollux.nss.nima.mil/pubs/ and scroll down the main page to find the link for needed information. The following may be downloaded (Note: Many of the resources are only available in digital format):

USCG Light List: Current information on location and status of maintained navigational aids.

Chart No. 1: Nautical Chart Symbols Abbreviations and Terms. The reference chart that explains all! Free download is large.

NGA List of Lights: Worldwide version of the USCG list.

NOAA Office of Coast Survey

This site is a useful one for information on waterways anywhere in the United States. The Coast Survey holds the distinction of being the oldest scientific organization in the United States, founded in 1807. For electronic chart locations, views, and download or mail sales, click on the prominent icon titled, "Electronic Navigational Charts." Electronic charts are updated at least once a month for current *Notices to Mariners.* Note: many computer programs and GPS receivers use proprietary charts; therefore, you may not be able to use these.

http://nauticalcharts.noaa.gov/

NOAA Main Page for Charting and Navigation

This site gives you access to many areas of NOAA, including current and historical charts, tide and current tables, etc.

http://www.noaa.gov/charts.html

Topo Zone

This is a very useful site. The company has worked with the U.S. Geological Survey (USGS) to create interactive topographic maps of the entire United States! They also carry every USGS topographic map, orthophotomap, and aerial photograph covering the entire United States. As topo maps often are better than nautical charts for near-coastal navigation, this could be an often-used resource.

http://www.topozone.com/

Waterproof Charts, Inc.

This company produces a variety of accurate charts on synthetic paper. Updated and current, the charts include easily read GPS coordinates.

http://www.waterproofcharts.com/

Maptech, Inc.

The Maptech site includes selection of waterproof charts, as well as waterproof guides to on-water chart symbols and GPS use for on-water navigation.

http://www.maptech.com/water/

University of California Alexandria Project

University of California, Santa Barbara site, still in final development at the time of this writing, will allow access to any and all digital maps, photographs, etc., related to a specific location. Try the Gazetteer link first. Because the site is still undergoing beta testing, sessions are timed and comments are welcomed and may influence the continued development of this resource.

http://www.alexandria.ucsb.edu/

WEATHER INFORMATION

FNMOC

When on the ocean, wave height may give an indication of safe landing zones, changes in shoreline dynamics, or suitability for safe passage. Other raw meteorological data can be useful for predicting weather trends or changing sea states. The Fleet Numerical Meteorology and Oceanography Center—FNMOC—is a U.S. Department of Defense site. It is full of data and not the easiest to navigate. It provides a wealth of remote sensing (read: satellite/drone/buoy) information from anywhere in the world. If you're a weather-techie, this is your site! Sorry, but we as kayakers are only allowed to access the unclassified areas of this site. Prominent warnings indicate the site may become restricted due to security concerns. Do not fool around on this site. You may be visited by people who have no sense of humor.

> https://www.fnmoc.navy.mil/

NOAA/NWS National Data Buoy Center

This site allows you to access and track real-time weather and sea-state information from automatic buoys in U.S., Canadian, and selected foreign waters; all of definite interest to those who plan offshore or coastal trips.

> http://www.ndbc.noaa.gov/

National Weather Service

NOAA and the National Weather Service (NWS) provide continually updated reports for land and marine environments. Lots of interesting information and easily navigated. For marine weather, scan the left margin and click on Marine under the heading Forecasts. Incidentally, this is the same forecast available through your VHF radio but without the monotonous robotic voices.

> www.weather.gov

GENERAL INTEREST AND INFORMATION

St. Cronan's School

Located in Bray, Co. Wicklow, Ireland, this is a primary school for boys "aged from about 7 to 12." For some reason, they have an excellent page on tides, currents, and why these phenomena occur. Nicely done graphic explanations with some good links to trustworthy sites.

> http://homepage.eircom.net/~cronews/geog/tides/tide.html

What causes the tides?

By Rick Groleau/NOVA-PBS, this is a fascinating site, enhanced by Flash-animated graphic representation of this phenomenon.

http://www.pbs.org/wgbh/nova/venice/tides.html

Rules of Navigation

U.S. Dept. of Transportation/U.S. Coast Guard PDF-format downloadable *Rules of the Nautical Road* for all inland and international mariners.

http://www.uscg.mil/vtm/navrules/navrules.pdf

Trimble Navigation Site: GPS Overview and Use

This commercial site has an easy-to-understand tutorial for beginning GPS users who need to understand the mechanics of GPS.

http://www.trimble.com/gps/

Marina Locater: Marinas.com

This site may be useful for either planned or unplanned trips. Marinas often have bathrooms, ship's stores, and repair facilities that kayakers may find useful.

http://www.marinas.com/

Starpath Navigation Courses

Starpath is a well-known name in small craft navigation and offers online and home-study courses that may reinforce your knowledge. Offering celestial, coastal, weather, and emergency course curriculums among others, the many satisfied users of these online programs testify to their appropriateness. The site also offers a nice store for navigation reference materials and equipment.

http://www.starpath.com/

Celestial Navigation Net

Celestial navigation is the art and science of finding your way by the sun, moon, stars, and planets, and it requires few or no batteries. This web page is a virtual clearinghouse for information related to the art of celestial navigation. Many interesting lessons, historical perspectives, and links.

http://www.celestialnavigation.net/

The American Canoe Association

A national organization designed to promote safety, instruction, conservation, and competition for all paddling disciplines.

http://www.acanet.org/

NAVIGATION EQUIPMENT

Weems and Plath, Inc.

Weems and Plath is a manufacturer of navigation tools.

http://www.weems-plath.com/

Problems and Answers in Navigation and Piloting

Written by Elbert S. Maloney, 1985. (ISBN: 0870211501), this book provides a foundation and practice problems in piloting, dead reckoning, and celestial navigation. Available through NavRules site. Click Navigation Publications on left side of the page, then scroll down to the book. Available through major retailers also.

http://www.navrules.com/

Boatingvideos.com

This site offers navigational instructional videos and DVDs covering celestial navigation, the use of nautical charts, coastal piloting, basic coastal navigation, etc.

http://www.boatingvideos.com/

The Small Craft Nav-Aid

Designed by Dr. Chuck Sutherland, this simple tool comes with an instructional booklet and helps kayakers and small boat sailors accurately determine bearings from charts while underway. It's cheap ($8.00), bomb-proof, and works! Mail orders only. When on the site, click on Main Page, then choose Cold Water from the top right icon for vital information on hypothermia accidents, prevention, and treatment. Dr. Sutherland is the main investigator of cold-water-related kayak and canoe accidents and deaths.

http://www.enter.net/~skimmer/coastal.html

Navigation Aid Course Conversion Calculator

Made of plastic, this calculator has two rotating compass cards with index marks and a rectangular relative bearing indicator. By rotating the various components, you can determine true and compass courses, as well as true bearings from relative. It also converts true course to magnetic course and compass course. And it does all of these calculations without the use of a pencil and at a cost of only $18.95. Other products, including instructional videos and courses, are offered as well on the site.

http://www.navigationaid.com/

Unit Conversions

Conversions below are rounded:

Unit		Conversion
League	=	3 nautical miles
	=	3.45 statute miles
	=	3,036 fathoms
	=	5,552.24 meters
	=	6,072 yards
	=	18,216 feet
Nautical mile	=	1.15 statute miles
	=	1,012.67 fathoms
	=	1,852 meters
	=	2,026 yards
	=	6,076 feet
Statute mile	=	0.87 nautical miles
	=	880 fathoms
	=	1,609 meters
	=	1,760 yards
	=	5,280 feet
Cable	=	100 fathoms
	=	182.88 meters
	=	200 yards
	=	600 feet
Fathom	=	6 feet

Index